BC525C

Canovan.

G. K. Chesterton.

G. K. Chesterton

Radical Populist

Also by Margaret Canovan

The Political Thought of Hannah Arendt

G. K. Chesterton

Radical Populist

Margaret Canovan

HARCOURT BRACE JOVANOVICH

NEW YORK AND LONDON

Printed in the United States of America

Library of Congress Cataloging in Publication Data

Canovan, Margaret.
G. K. Chesterton: radical populist.

Bibliography: p.
Includes index.
1. Chesterton, Gilbert Keith, 1873–1936—
Political and social views. 2. Populism.
PR4453.C4Z582   828′.9′1209   77–73045
ISBN 0–15–135700–5

First edition

B C D E

Acknowledgments

I am indebted to Miss Dorothy Collins for permission to quote from Chesterton's works, and also to the following publishers for permission to make extensive quotations from specific works: to The Bodley Head and to Dodd, Mead & Company for *Orthodoxy* by G. K. Chesterton, copyright 1908 by Dodd, Mead & Company, copyright renewed 1935 by Gilbert K. Chesterton; and to Dodd, Mead & Company for *The Collected Poems of G.K. Chesterton,* copyright 1932 by Dodd, Mead & Company, Inc., copyright renewed 1959 by Oliver Chesterton. I am also grateful for help from Russell Price, who allowed me to read his unpublished dissertation on Hilaire Belloc's *The Servile State,* and from April Carter, who read the first draft of this book and made many helpful suggestions. My greatest debt is to my husband, who first aroused my interest in Chesterton, and who has read and criticized successive drafts with unfailing patience, insight, and tact.

Contents

5

G. K.
Chesterton

Radical Populist

1

An English Populist

If you ask me whether I think the populace, especially the poor, should be recognized as citizens who can rule the state, I answer in a voice of thunder, "Yes."[1]

The political traditions of even the freest countries are always limited. The range of standpoints represented within the mainstream of political thought and activity in even the most pluralist state never covers the whole spectrum of intelligible political attitudes. Foreigners have often remarked on the conspicuous absence of any strong socialist tradition in American politics, but a corresponding gap in English* political culture has passed virtually unnoticed. Perhaps one reason for this is that the political standpoints that have been influential in modern English history can be fitted together into a neat pattern, which is so coherent that it looks misleadingly comprehensive. At the right of the traditional English spectrum stands the Conservative, who represents patriotism and the preservation of traditional arrangements, among them inequality of wealth. On his left is the Liberal, who is primarily concerned with freedom, and who varies in his political affinities according as he concerns himself chiefly with free-

---

* The term "English" has been chosen in preference to "British" because Chesterton always thought of himself as an Englishman, and because English attitudes and interests have dominated British politics. Specifically Scottish, Welsh, and especially Irish political traditions have been significantly different from English ones in many respects.

dom of property or with "positive freedom," the extension of opportunity. To the left of the Liberal stands the Socialist, who is primarily concerned with social welfare, and who may be nearer to or farther away from the Liberal, according to the amount of state control he thinks necessary to obtain it.

This picture of the political spectrum is so familiar to Englishmen, and looks so coherent and rational, that it is easy to suppose it all-embracing. Any other possible political position, it is assumed, must be either to the right of the Tory (which heaven forbid) or to the left of the Socialist (a situation appropriate only to the idealistic young). Yet there is at least one other characteristic political outlook which is left out of this canon altogether, and which defies classification within it.

We shall find it easier to recognize this neglected brand of politics if we look more closely at a characteristic common to those brands familiar to Englishmen: their lack of egalitarianism. It goes without saying that English conservatism is elitist. Since ceasing to believe in rule by blood, Conservatives have come to believe in rule by ability, but they could never in any case have been attracted by the ideal of equality. What is more remarkable is the degree to which the same is true of English liberalism and English socialism. The patron saint of English liberalism, John Stuart Mill, could put forward schemes for plural voting by the more educated, in order that the enlightened should rule, while the most influential version of English socialism has been Fabianism —rule by skilled administrators in the people's best interest.

In other words, the great gap in the modern English political spectrum—as startling as the virtual absence of socialism in America—is the lack of radical democracy. This is curious when one remembers the Chartists, the Levellers, or the medieval peasants who chanted: "When Adam delved and Eve span / Who was then the gentleman?" England, however, is a great exception in modern history in having no significant class of small proprietors, so it is perhaps not surprising that the political attitudes that have tended to appeal widely to peasants and small craftsmen

4

have been lacking. For the gap in the spectrum is that amorphous but recognizable collection of political views that is usually called populism.

Like liberalism, socialism, conservatism, or any other complex political phenomenon, populism is impossible to define and difficult to characterize.[2] The two classic cases from which the name comes down to us indicate the range of political movements to which it can refer, for they were the American Populist Party of the 1890s, and the Russian Narodniki of the 1860s and 1870s. In the American case we have a constitutionally organized political party formed mainly of small farmers, demanding government action to redress their concrete economic grievances; in Russia, a loose network of clandestine groups of revolutionary intellectuals who projected on to an unresponsive peasantry their anarchistic visions of social justice. In one of the most interesting recent attempts to characterize populism, Professor Peter Wiles has called it "A Syndrome, not a Doctrine."[3] Identifying as the major premise, "Virtue resides in the simple people, who are the overwhelming majority, and in their collective traditions," he goes on to set up an ideal type with a long list of characteristics, and to stress that many actual cases do not conform to the type in all respects. The twenty-four elements of his ideal-type include, among other things, opposition to governing elites, financiers, and intellectuals ("Even its intellectuals try to be anti-intellectual"); an economic model of producers' co-operatives, opposed equally to large-scale capitalism and to socialism; a reverence for religion and a suspicion of science and progress; and "mild racialism." Professor Wiles stresses that "there is a range of populisms, from the pre-industrial, anti-industrial 'peasant' strain to the affluent industry-tolerating 'farmer' strain."[4]

While it would be rash, therefore, to attempt any rigid definition of populism, it is certainly a recognizable political standpoint. At its heart lies always a faith in the common sense of ordinary, hard-working people, especially country people, and an intense suspicion of metropolitan society, plutocrats, bureaucrats,

5

and intellectuals. Populists are usually tradition-minded advocates of the simple virtues of country life; they are often fierce defenders of small property, though hostile to the landlords, moneylenders, and other intruders who threaten the small farmer's security. They dislike complex arrangements and subtle compromises, and have the outsider's distrust of professional politicians. They are generally regarded as a reactionary force in politics, and it is perhaps only natural that the intellectuals whom they despise should have usually returned the compliment.

Compared with other political movements, populists have had a bad press. The Russian populists labor under the disadvantage of having failed utterly, so that it is all too easy to assume that their failure was inevitable, to regard them as reactionaries from a dying class, or to explain away their attitudes in psychological terms.[5] The American Populists, denouncing the financial tyranny of Eastern bankers from their strongholds in the West and South, were never looked upon with great favor by Eastern intellectuals, and during the McCarthyite scare after World War II it became customary for liberal intellectuals to see populism as a progenitor of fascism and an expression of dark, irrational emotions. More recently the pendulum has swung back somewhat, and several American scholars have defended the Populists against this aspersion of fascism.[6] Nevertheless, it is true to say that even in the United States, where populist traditions are still a force in politics, populism has a less distinct and less favorable image in intellectual circles than most other political standpoints.

As we suggested initially, the situation in England is even worse, for even the name is unfamiliar. Consequently, those few English political writers and agitators who have worked out for themselves what is in effect a populist standpoint, have tended to be embarrassed for want of a name and a party to join. The classic case is that of William Cobbett, a pure populist, defender of the small farmer against the landlords, the Establishment, and the Industrial Revolution. It is instructive that Cobbett began life as a Tory and ended as a Radical, without being pleased by his company in either case. The Chartist movement had many populist characteristics; but after the triumph of industrialization in England in the mid-nineteenth century, English populists are few and far between. This book is about one of the most interesting of them, G. K. Chesterton.

Many of Chesterton's readers, knowing him chiefly as the author of the Father Brown detective stories, will be surprised to hear that he had any political views at all. Yet even the Father Brown stories, considered in themselves, provide clues from which an armchair detective could infer a characteristic political outlook. To begin with, Chesterton's detective is himself quite without the glamor of most such fictional figures. Far from being a brooding genius, like Holmes, or a sophisticated ladies' man given to dropping Shakespearean quotations, like many of the heroes of the great age of the detective story, he is a small, clumsy, insignificant parish priest—not even a Jesuit. While the mysteries he solves are sometimes set in high life, they characteristically end in the exposure of some particularly eminent and respectable member of the Establishment as the criminal. Unlike most fictional detectives, however, Father Brown does not turn his criminals over to the police, having a firm belief in God's justice and an anarchic distrust of secular law.

An ecclesiastical investigator, particularly a Catholic one, might perhaps be expected to attribute the crimes he investigates to mysterious and occult causes. But as a matter of fact, Father Brown's speciality is sheer common sense, which continually enables him to expose the superstition of supposedly "scientific" experts. His distrust of progress as represented by science extends also to modern business and its worldwide imperialism. On one occasion a rather improbable excursion to Latin America gives him an opportunity to side with the supposedly benighted peasants of a "backward" country against the progressive forces of Yankee capitalism. Above all, Father Brown is able to solve mysteries because he sees men as equal human beings, stripped of their secular dignities. One story, for instance, hinges on the fact that he actually pays attention to a waiter—a man who is virtually invisible to the gentlemen in the same room, because they see him as part of the furniture.[7]

Even in the Father Brown stories, then, Chesterton shows a characteristically populist outlook—something that he went on to develop throughout his multifarious writings. We shall attempt to piece together and describe this outlook, with two purposes in mind. The first is simply to contribute to the proper understanding of Chesterton as a thinker and writer. Chesterton has never lacked readers, who continue to be attracted by the ingenuity of his stories and the characteristic combination of brilliance and sanity in his essays. However, his political views must have mystified many English readers, because they fall outside the ordinary range of political choice in England. He was well aware of this himself, but his attempts to persuade his countrymen that it was they who were out of step fell upon deaf ears.

The primary aim of this book, then, is to present a side of Chesterton's thought that has been unduly neglected. The second, while subsidiary, is perhaps more ambitious: to urge the claims of populism to more serious consideration among the political standpoints now available. In England, as we have seen, populism has simply gone unnoticed: but even in countries familiar with it as a political force, such as America, it is rarely treated seriously as an intellectual position. This is understandable, since with the exception of Russia, where it was actually invented and propagated by intellectuals, populism has usually been an antiintellectual standpoint, held by comparatively uneducated people and not intellectually worked out.

Chesterton's own position was somewhat paradoxical. In the first place, he was himself a populist intellectual, although of a thoroughly antiintellectualist kind. Furthermore, although he had a vast and loyal readership, it is doubtful how many of his readers shared his political views. He set out to speak to and for the common man, but there was never any specific group or class of the people whom he represented or whose grievances he articulated.

When he did eventually become involved in a political movement, Distributism, his position was particularly anomalous: for while the aim of Distributism was the typically populist one of small property for all, the movement was an attempt to *create* a peasantry, not to represent one. As a result, the Distributist League itself became another of those bands of eccentric ladies and gentlemen, purveying their esoteric solutions to the problems of the poor, that Chesterton had ridiculed in the case of teetotalers and Tolstoyans.

It is easy to dwell on the absurdity of a populist without a people. However, in some ways Chesterton's position as a free-floating intellectual outside all political parties was actually an advantage to his clarity of thought. Populists who emerge from some active popular movement to articulate conscious popular grievances are no doubt stronger in political realism, but their thinking is often limited by the demands of the specific situation, as the American Populists of the late nineteenth century were by their preoccupation with currency reform. Coherent social theories are more often worked out by those not deeply involved with any such movement; as we shall see, Chesterton went exceptionally far toward articulating in coherent form the characteristic values of populists.

His writings have all the frequently noticed vices of populism: the outsider's ignorance of the complexities of politics and his distrust of compromise; the hostility to professional politicians that can lead to support for a popular dictator; the attraction to conspiracy theories, putting all the blame for modern evils on a ring of international plutocrats; even, deplorably, the antisemitism. These defects of populism have often been pointed out. What is less frequently noticed, however, is that populism also has its characteristic virtues, and of these Chesterton's writings are a shining example. At the heart of these virtues is a respect for the humanity and dignity of ordinary, shabby, ignorant people, and a refusal to be impressed by the claims of wealth and cleverness. Coupled with this is a concern for those things that matter not to a few intellectuals but to the mass of the people, like a home and a family; also—linked to this concern—the cool evaluation of "progress" in terms of its impact on the common man, and the refusal to be stampeded by an elite who regard themselves as the vanguard of history. In defense of values like these, Chesterton developed a political stance that was thoroughly radical while being utterly opposed to socialism. One of the subsidiary purposes of this book is to stress the obvious but often forgotten truth that radicalism need not mean socialism, and that a disbelief in Marxism need not imply acceptance of social injustice.

. . .

Gilbert Keith Chesterton was born in London on May 29, 1874, of solid middle-class stock, the son of a house agent with a well-established and respectable family business. As he later remarked in his *Autobiography*,[8] "One peculiarity of this middle-class is that it really was a class and it really was in the middle" equally distinct from the aristocrats and millionaires of London society, and from the working classes whom it knew mainly as servants. From this background he absorbed a traditional liberalism, much of which he was to retain all his life in spite of his later dissatisfaction with the Liberal Party. He also inherited a vestigial and undogmatic version of Christianity, a considerable depth of literary culture, and an abiding respect for domesticity. His father possessed means and leisure, and the imagination and energy to make use of them, pouring his talents into a variety of hobbies, above all into the production of plays in a toy theater. These dramas in miniature typified for Chesterton the rich world of his childhood, and in later years, looking back on that continual flow of happy activity, he poured scorn on the supposed dullness and constriction of family life.

The years of Chesterton's youth saw the passing of the classic two-party phase of British politics, when parliamentary business had seemed an epic struggle between the mighty figures of Gladstone and Disraeli. Under Parnell, the large contingent of Irish

MPs became a political force that could not be ignored, and in 1886 the Liberals split over the question of Home Rule for Ireland, the Unionists who opposed it eventually joining forces with the Conservatives. From the 1890s, also, the labor movement began to emerge in party politics, although for many years socialist influence was exerted more effectively outside Parliament, at the grass roots through the rapid growth of trade unionism, and in elite circles by the Fabian Society, founded in 1884 and dominated by Sidney and Beatrice Webb. Like many idealistic young men of his time, Chesterton was initially drawn to socialism, although he was soon to find himself out of sympathy with most of his Fabian friends. As yet, however, both the main political parties remained overwhelmingly aristocratic in their personnel; concern with class conflict and social justice were not salient issues in British politics, which was dominated instead by the recurrent problem of Ireland and the periodic crises engendered by imperial expansion overseas. The most notable of these was the Boer War, which broke out in 1899 and dragged on until 1902.

The Boer War was the first political issue regarding which Chesterton found himself taking up an emphatic personal position. The war was very popular in England, at any rate as long as victory seemed easy, and jingoism swept the country. A large section of the Liberal Party supported it as strongly as the Conservative/Unionist government, and so did the majority of the Fabian Socialists, among them Chesterton's brother Cecil. The only large body of MPs who opposed the war were the Irish Nationalists, whose anti-British sympathy with the Boers naturally did nothing to make the Boer cause popular in England. To be against the war in 1899 was in fact to be labeled a traitor, an enemy to patriotism. Chesterton found himself in the company of a small group holding this unpopular position, and he later explained his feelings in his *Autobiography*. He found, he said, that he belonged to "a minority of a minority." Most of those Liberals and Socialists who opposed the war, did so on grounds of general humanitarian idealism: because they were pacifists who disapproved of all fighting, and internationalists who regarded patriotism as a destructive force. Chesterton found that he had little in common with most of his allies:

I emphatically was a Pro-Boer, and I emphatically was not a pacifist. My point was that the Boers were right in fighting; not that anybody must be wrong in fighting. I thought that their farmers were perfectly entitled to take to horse and rifle in defence of their farms, and their little farming common wealth, when it was invaded by a more cosmopolitan empire at the command of very cosmopolitan financiers.[9]

He had in fact become aware of a distinction upon which he was later to lay great stress. It was the distinction between patriotism and imperialism: between, on the one hand, the willingness to defend one's home and way of life—which can extend to a sympathy with the patriotisms of other nations—and on the other hand, the attempt to extend power (especially financial power) over the world, crushing other people's homes in the process. In particular, Chesterton objected that too many of the British *Uitlanders* in South Africa, in whose defense the war was supposedly fought, were not Britons at all, but Jews, for the sake of whose financial interests the struggle was being carried on. We shall have occasion later to consider this attitude to Jews in Chesterton's political thought.

The minority of radical and pro-Boer Liberals with whom Chesterton was associated took over a weekly, *The Speaker,* and Chesterton began to write regularly for it on a wide variety of subjects. He and his readers quickly discovered that he had a natural flair for journalism. His style was lively, pointed, amusing, and immensely readable, and he could write on the most unpromising subjects—in defense of "Rash Vows" or "Penny Dreadfuls," for instance—and say something that was not only entertaining but original, striking, and sane. Above all, his writings were marked by the vigor with which he attacked the whole varied intellectual establishment of his time and challenged its authority.

12

One of the resounding successes of these early years was *Heretics,* published in 1905, in which Chesterton took on most of the literary heroes of his day, from Wells and Shaw to Kipling and Tolstoy, and maintained that each was in his own way a heretic— "that is to say, a man whose philosophy is quite solid, quite coherent, and quite wrong."[10] He set out to demonstrate the deficiencies of these various personal philosophies, and in doing so began to sketch in his own 'orthodoxy', which he elaborated in a book of that title published in 1908: the blend of Christianity, populism, and common sense that became his characteristic standpoint and unites all the articles and books that poured from his pen for the rest of his life.

A glance at a bibliography of Chesterton's works indicates the bewildering variety of subjects on which he wrote. Besides his extremely miscellaneous essays, and his works of political and religious controversy, he wrote a great deal of literary criticism, poetry, novels, stories, travel books, and studies ranging from a book on G. F. Watts's painting to another on Thomas Aquinas's theology. The skeptical reader will at once suspect that most of these must have been very superficial, and there are certainly grounds for this view. One of the first of his books to gain widespread recognition was his study of Browning, published in 1903, and the story of its reception is instructive. It was hailed by most reviewers for its brilliance, originality, and penetrating insight— and simultaneously condemned for its lack of scholarship. For instance, Chesterton had quoted from memory, and his memory— though prodigious—was not always accurate. He had misquoted a great many of Browning's lines; staggeringly, he had even unconsciously invented a new line for Browning's poem "Mr. Sludge the Medium."

During the early years of the century, when Chesterton was building a reputation as a lively and individual writer, he was also gradually clarifying his political position. He soon left behind the youthful phase of socialism, but it took him much longer to work out his relations with liberalism. He never ceased to think of himself as a Liberal, and he canvassed for Liberal parliamentary candidates in the elections of 1902 and 1906. For many years he wrote regularly for the Liberal newspaper, the *Daily News,* owned by Mr. Cadbury of Cadbury's Cocoa, although his situation there became increasingly incongruous. The Liberal readers of the newspaper were mostly members of the Nonconformist middle class, teetotal, semipacifist, insular believers in progress and enlightenment. But Chesterton's views, aided by the influence of his friend Hilaire Belloc, were moving in a quite different direction—toward an agrarian populism colored by the traditional outlook of the nationalistic, wine-drinking, Catholic peasantry of France, Belloc's ancestral country on his mother's side. As early as 1908, Chesterton's brother Cecil scoffed at his connection with the *Daily News:* "Thousands of peaceful semi-Tolstoian Nonconformists have for six years been compelled to listen every Saturday morning to a fiery apostle preaching...War, Drink and Catholicism."[11]*

Chesterton's eventual break with the *Daily News* was symptomatic of his increasing dissatisfaction with the Liberal Party, which seemed to him to have ceased to defend freedom. The occasion of his disillusionment was the program of "social reform" implemented by the Liberal government that took office in 1906, and we shall look in considerably more detail later at the reasons for Chesterton's opposition to it. At first sight, it seems puzzling that a radical populist should oppose such measures as Lloyd George's Insurance Act—did not these reforms lay the foundations of the welfare state? But what Chesterton objected to was the conversion of the Liberal Party to a form of tyrannical paternalism, represented as much by the Insurance Act as by the prohibition movement: a desire to do good to the poor against their will. Liberals, once the defenders of freedom, were now compulsorily educating the poor, sending health inspectors into their homes, endeavoring to control their drinking habits, taking away by force

---

* Chesterton was at this stage a High Church Anglican; he did not become a Roman Catholic until 1922.

14

their "defective" children, and obliging them to contribute to insurance funds over which they had no control.

We are so used to regarding measures of this kind as laudable reforms that it is hard to understand the position of those radicals who opposed them. It is important to grasp that in all these cases of compulsory reforms imposed in the name of the New Liberalism, the compulsion extended only to the working classes, and was exercised by the upper and middle classes, together with the new bureaucratic armies of teachers, health visitors, and civil servants of all kinds. As Lloyd George himself said, "If these poor people are to be redeemed they must be redeemed not by themselves . . . they must be redeemed by others outside."[12]

It was this benevolent despotism, exercised by men who called themselves Liberals, that was Chesterton's bugbear. As he remarked, "The philanthropist is not a brother, he is a supercilious aunt."[13] He opposed to this species of covert elitism a different kind of liberalism—freedom for the poor—and elaborated his position in a book published in 1910, *What's Wrong with the World*. There he maintained that what the ordinary man in the street actually wanted and needed, had anyone troubled to ask him, was not regimentation and petty tyranny in the name of social reform, but simply a house and some small property of his own, within which he could live his own life and exercise the traditional liberal freedoms just as the upper and middle classes did.

Chesterton's opposition to the New Liberalism was influenced and strengthened by his friendship with Hilaire Belloc, who stated his own position in a celebrated book published in 1912: *The Servile State*. Belloc argued there that the new Liberal legislation, such as the Insurance Act, was in effect part of a trend toward the reinstatement of slavery, under which the proletariat would be compelled by law to work for their masters as the price of guaranteed material security. His point was that while no one explicitly intended such an outcome, the logic of the situation was tending to bring it about. High-minded philanthropic social reformers like the Webbs were, in principle, in favor of expropriating the rich as well as disciplining the poor; but the latter aim was feasible, whereas the former was not. Consequently, social reforms would leave the proletariat more than ever at the mercy of their employers, who would have all the backing of a bureaucratic state. Belloc's alternative to this threat of a fascist future was Distributism—the deliberate encouragement of small property ownership by as many people as possible. Chesterton was to adopt this idea and incorporate it into his own brand of populism.

Belloc had actually been elected as a Liberal MP in 1906, and his erratic career as a wayward backbencher, perpetually at odds with his own government, did much to strengthen Chesterton's own dissatisfaction with current party politics. In *Orthodoxy* Chesterton had written, "As much as I ever did, more than I ever did, I believe in Liberalism. But there was a rosy time of innocence when I believed in Liberals."[14] Closer acquaintance with the political process soon disillusioned him. He records in his *Autobiography*[15] how, while electioneering, he noticed that the parliamentary candidate was often very much less able than his supporters. The paradox was easily resolved: the candidate had achieved his position not through his ability, still less because he was representative of the ordinary citizen, but through his wealth and connections; Chesterton concluded, "What runs modern politics is money." In 1907 Campbell-Bannerman, the Liberal leader, was criticized in Parliament for selling peerages in return for subscriptions to secret party funds, and Chesterton promptly wrote an article roundly condemning such transactions. However, when he sent his article off to the *Daily News,* he ran up against the exigencies of party politics. The editor explained that he could not print the article, not because he disagreed with it, but because "just at this moment it would look like backing Lea's unmannerly attack on C.B."[16] In other words, loyalty to the party came first.

Chesterton's political stance at this time was closely connected with those of his friend Belloc and his brother Cecil Chesterton. In 1911 these two collaborated to write *The Party System,* the outcome of Belloc's souring experiences in the House of Commons. The thesis of the book was that parliamentary democracy in Britain was a sham, since the front benches of the two main parties were merely branches of a single interrelated oligarchy, co-operating behind the scenes to share out the spoils of office. *The Party System* caused quite a stir, and the authors managed to raise the money to start a nonparty weekly, the *Eye Witness* (renamed the *New Witness* in 1912). Among other activities, the paper unearthed and kept before the public eye some dubious dealings in shares of the Marconi radio company by Lloyd George and other members of the government, and some even more dubious statements about the affair made by ministers to the House of Commons.[17] The ministers were officially cleared by a parliamentary enquiry, and in 1913 Cecil Chesterton was tried for libel, found guilty, and fined £100—an experience which confirmed his view of party politics. G. K. Chesterton was not himself involved in the affair, but his sympathies were with his brother, and he was shocked by the tricky and evasive tactics of the ministers concerned.

When Cecil went off to the war in 1916, Chesterton took over the editorship of the *New Witness,* to which he had been contributing regularly for some time. He himself was not fit enough to join the army, but he was an ardent supporter of World War I, regarding Britain's part in it as just, unlike her action against the Boers. He saw the war as a defensive struggle against Prussian aggression, and continued to hold this view in the postwar years, when many former patriots had reacted in disillusionment. He remarked in his *Autobiography,* "Those who now think too little of the Allied Cause are those who once thought too much of it." For instance, H. G. Wells had in his initial enthusiasm gone so far as to call it "the War That Will End War." Chesterton commented: "To tell a soldier defending his country that it is The War That Will End War is exactly like telling a workman, naturally rather reluctant to do his day's work, that it is The Work That Will End Work."[18] His own war effort consisted in writing propaganda pamphlets: *The Barbarism of Berlin* and *The Crimes of England*. (The latter "crimes" included having helped to make Prussia strong in the past, instead of siding with France.)

Chesterton had originally intended only to act as a temporary editor during his brother's absence. But Cecil died in a military hospital, and he felt obliged to carry on the paper as a kind of memorial. Its tone continued to be populist, concentrating on criticism of professional politicians and corruption in high places, defense of the poor against bureaucratic regimentation, and advocacy of property for all. The paper was chronically inefficient and short of funds, for Chesterton was no businessman. In 1925 it was reconstituted as *G.K.'s Weekly,* and from it grew Distributism.

The Distributist League was inaugurated by a meeting in London in September 1926. Chesterton explained that its aim was to restore property to ordinary people by encouraging small holdings, small shops, and self-employed craftsmen, as against big businesses and large landowners. The League was intended as a propaganda organ rather than an action group, and Chesterton in particular propagated its Distributist ideas through articles in *G.K.'s Weekly,* a collection of which was published in 1926 as *The Outline of Sanity*. At first the League spread quickly, and branches appeared in Birmingham, Manchester, Glagow, and other places. However, it soon suffered the fate of so many other such movements: instead of doing anything, the members talked incessantly, and quickly began to quarrel over the precise features of that Distributist Utopia that was nowhere in sight.

Another sore point concerned the relations between Catholic and non-Catholic Distributists, for in 1922 Chesterton had at last joined Belloc in the Roman Catholic Church. His conversion, which received a great deal of publicity, helped to foster the impression that there was something specifically and exclusively Catholic about the political principles that he and Belloc held— although Chesterton had already held them for nearly twenty years before his conversion.

18

In the intervals of editing *G.K.'s Weekly* and overseeing the activities and rivalries of the Distributist League, Chesterton continued to write with unabated energy until his death in 1936. He was in great demand as a lecturer and debater, and his speaking engagements and holidays overseas led to a series of travel books, including *Irish Impressions, What I Saw in America, The New Jerusalem,* and *The Resurrection of Rome.* The last of these, which contains an extremely ambivalent discussion of Mussolini's Fascism, will demand our attention later.

It is clear from a brief survey of Chesterton's life that, in spite of his political journalism and his fairly frequent appearances on public platforms, he cannot be regarded as a political figure. He was once asked after a lecture, "If you were Prime Minister, what would you do?"—to which he replied without a moment's hesitation, "If I were Prime Minister I should resign."[19] In earnest as in jest, he was no politician. He was a thinker and writer, and our concern in this book will be with the universe of ideas within which his political attitudes had their place. We shall begin in the next chapter by describing his intellectual antiintellectualism, the way in which his whole mode of thought was colored by his populist sympathy for the standpoint of the common man.

2

The Man Who
Discovered England

Orthodoxy, a book which Chesterton described as "a sort of slovenly autobiography," begins with a striking parable:

I have often had a fancy for writing a romance about an English yachtsman who slightly miscalculated his course and discovered England under the impression that it was a new island in the South Seas. . . . There will probably be a general impression that the man who landed (armed to the teeth and talking by signs) to plant the British flag on that barbaric temple which turned out to be the Pavilion at Brighton, felt rather a fool. I am not here concerned to deny that he looked a fool. But if you imagine that he felt a fool, or at any rate that the sense of folly was his sole or his dominant emotion, then you have not studied with sufficient delicacy the rich romantic nature of the hero of this tale. His mistake was really a most enviable mistake; and he knew it, if he was the man I take him for. What could be more delightful than to have in the same few minutes all the fascinating terrors of going abroad combined with all the humane security of coming home again? . . .

But I have a peculiar reason for mentioning the man in a yacht, who discovered England. For I am that man in a yacht. I discovered England.[1]

In this parable Chesterton related his attempts to formulate a philosophy of life from his own experience, and his eventual discovery—both deflating and reassuring—that what he had discovered after all his efforts was the doctrine of the Christian Church. The story of the yachtsman, which sums up so neatly Chesterton's account of his religious evolution, provides us with an excellent point of departure from which we can explore his manner of thought, and what we have termed his populism. For the peculiar character of Chesterton's thought was that it was on the one hand extremely personal, if not idiosyncratic, and marked by freshness and originality; while on the other hand its conclusions were notable for their common-sense sanity, and were particularly likely to support traditional and popular views against the ideas of the intellectual elite. Not only in his religious evolution, but in his thought on all manner of subjects, Chesterton followed a train of thought of idiosyncratic originality to a common-sense conclusion—like his yachtsman who sailed the seven seas to discover England.

Early in his career Chesterton became famous—and indeed notorious—for his constant use of paradox. There is a tendency, particularly in his later works, for the paradoxes to become the overworked tricks of a tired writer. Very often, however, his paradoxical statements really do bring out a neglected truth. But the most fundamental paradox of Chesterton's thought is to be found in the purposes for which he used such a style. We must remember that he came to maturity in the 1890s, and that he learned this mode of paradoxical witticism from Oscar Wilde. Significantly, however, he used this style to put forward not the exotic viewpoint of the Decadents, but what he took to be the outlook of the ordinary man.

Chesterton was a populist not merely in his specifically political opinions but in his whole outlook on life, for he deliberately used his own power of original thought, together with the paradoxical style of the intellectual elite, in order to defend against that elite the common sense of the common man. As he remarked in *Orthodoxy,* "If I have had a bias, it was always a bias in favour of democracy, and therefore of tradition. . . . I have always been more inclined to believe the ruck of hard-working people than to believe that special and troublesome literary class to which I belong."[2]

In order to appreciate the battle that Chesterton believed himself to be fighting, we must recall the intellectual climate in which he found himself. This was, on the one hand, the age of Decadence and exoticism. In the generally pessimistic metaphysical atmosphere, exotic semireligions like spiritualism and theosophy were fashionable: English writers imported from France the doctrine of Art for Art's sake, or from Germany the Nietzschean exaltation of the Will: above all, the gifted few felt themselves to be an elite with finer sensibilities, nobler blood, or higher natures than the masses.

On the other hand, meanwhile, serious scientific reformers, for all their concern about the "social problem," were not much more democratic. Their socialism, itself often a vision of authoritarian planning, was bound up with beliefs in materialistic determinism that were just as elitist, if more well-intentioned. Chesterton commented in *Orthodoxy* on the way in which these supposedly humane and progressive materialist beliefs undermined the ideal of equality:

I have listened often enough to Socialists, or even to democrats, saying that the physical conditions of the poor must of necessity make them mentally and morally degraded. I have listened to scientific men ... saying that if we give the poor healthier conditions vice and wrong will disappear. I have listened to them with a horrible attention, with a hideous fascination. For it was like watching a man energetically sawing from the tree the branch he is sitting on. If these happy democrats could prove their case, they would strike democracy dead. If the poor are thus utterly demoralised, it may or may not be practical to raise them. But it is certainly quite practical to disfranchise them. If the man with a bad bedroom cannot give a good vote, then the first and swiftest deduction is that he shall give no vote. The governing class may not unreasonably say, "It may take us some time to reform his bedroom. But if he is the brute you say, it will take him very little time to ruin our country. Therefore we will take your hint and not give him the chance." It fills me with horrible amusement to observe the way in which the earnest Socialist industriously lays the foundation of all aristocracy, expatiating blandly upon the evident unfitness of the poor to rule.[8]

It was in the context of beliefs like these that Chesterton saw himself as a crusader, fighting against the spirit of the age. Against the dominant intellectual current he defended a view of human nature and the human condition that favored the common man: a belief in the equality of men, and the vital importance of every single individual; a belief in free will versus determinism; in common sense and common morality against "progressive" thought; in the goodness of ordinary life against pessimism. The point of view for which he fought, that is to say, was at once a very personal one and one that seemed to him to belong to the generality of ordinary men, to be less narrow and more popular than the views of the intelligentsia.

Chesterton could perhaps be compared with the aristocratic Russian populists of the nineteenth century, or with Orwell on his pilgrimage to the industrial North of England. For while Chesterton did not give up riches to share the poverty of the people, he used his intellectual sophistication expressly to vindicate common sense against the elitist intellectual orthodoxy. A man who always loved a good argument, he enjoyed his constant running battle with the intellectuals, and went out of his way to defend the things that they scorned. We shall see this most clearly in his defenses of the home, the family, and peasant property, but it was a constant feature of his writing. Here he is, for instance, deflating the complex analyses of marital difficulties with which so many contemporary plays and novels were concerned, by attributing them to the idleness of a leisured class:

If two married people moon about in large rooms all day long, it is highly probable that they will get on each other's nerves. . . . half the affectionate couples of the world are perpetually parted lovers. An omnibus conductor and his wife see almost as little of each other as Romeo and Juliet. A postman and his chosen meet, if not secretly, at least by night."[4]

In his first volume of essays, *The Defendant,* Chesterton defended penny dreadfuls and detective stories, not just for the pleasure of being paradoxical, but in order to assert the validity of universal human tastes—which he himself enthusiastically shared—against a merely snobbish fastidiousness. It seems that, long before the modern debate on television and the causes of violence, magistrates were already attributing juvenile crime to the reading of penny dreadfuls, the blood-curdling comic papers of the time. Chesterton poured scorn upon this claim:

In this matter, as in all such matters, we lose our bearings entirely by speaking of the "lower classes" when we mean humanity minus ourselves. This trivial romantic literature is not especially plebeian: it is simply human. The philanthropist can never forget classes and callings. He says, with a modest swagger, "I have invited twenty-five factory hands to tea." If he said, "I have invited twenty-five chartered accountants to tea," everyone would see the humor of so simple a classification. But this is what we have done with this lumberland of foolish writing: we have probed, as if it were some monstrous new disease, what is, in fact, nothing but the foolish and valiant heart of man. Ordinary men will always be sentimentalists: for a sentimentalist is simply a man who has feelings and does not trouble to invent a new way of expressing them. These common and current publications have nothing essentially evil about them. They express the sanguine and heroic truisms on which civilisation is built; for it is clear that unless civilisation is built on truisms, it is not built at all. Clearly, there could be no safety for a society in which the remark by the Chief Justice that murder was wrong was regarded as an original and dazzling epigram.[5]

As he pointed out, if the police wanted to find what was sapping morality, they should seize the advanced novels of the literati, not the crude stories of the people.

Such defenses of popular taste against a self-appointed intellectual elite were part of Chesterton's consistent championship of

---

the standpoint of the common man. At times this championship took a somewhat quixotic turn, as when in *Orthodoxy*—partly for the pleasure of baiting the intellectuals—he treated fairy stories as repositories of profound truth about the human condition. Similarly, he appealed frequently from the stale world-weariness of the intellectual to the fresh and innocent vision of the child, with his insatiable delight in ordinary things. But Chesterton's fondness for using the child's viewpoint as a touch-stone of truth was not merely a way of deflating the pretensions of intellectuals; by considering his purpose, we can uncover a further aspect of his paradoxical mode of thought. As we have seen, he used the free reflections of his own educated mind in order to reject the fashionable fads of the intellectual establishment; but his purpose in doing so was not merely to reaffirm clichés, whether popular or not. The child's viewpoint is important because the child looks at things afresh, which enables him to see, not anything exotic or original, but something obvious that is hidden behind clichés.

This point, symbolized by the fresh vision of the child, was one of Chesterton's most constant preoccupations. It seemed to him that men are often unable to see the world in which they live, or to appreciate their own feelings, simply because they are stale. He had himself been blessed with a more lively vision, and he struggled constantly in his books and essays to bring home to his readers the astonishing reality of their own experience. He deliberately used his capacity for free reflection in order to turn his back on intellectual fads and to recover common sense, yet this was not merely a matter of appealing from the few to the many. Instead, Chesterton took a longer route. He endeavored to see life anew, with the innocent vision of a child, and *thereby* to arrive at the same conclusions as the men who made the popular traditions he inherited. His object was to see things afresh, to make the effort of articulating direct experience, and yet to conclude, not with some exotic and original viewpoint, but by closing the circle in orthodoxy. This, evidently is something of an intellectual feat, and his method will be easier to understand if we look at his line of thought in *Orthodoxy* itself.

Published in 1908, *Orthodoxy** was written in response to a challenge. One of Chesterton's critics, reviewing *Heretics,* had said, "I will begin to worry about my philosophy when Mr. Chesterton has given us his." As Chesterton remarked, "It was perhaps an incautious suggestion to make to a person only too ready to write books upon the feeblest provocation."[6] The book begins with the parable of the yachtsman, indicating man's need to be "at once astonished at the world and yet at home in it,"[7] for its object was to articulate Chesterton's own experience of life and his reflections on the human condition, and to show how these led him to a philosophy of life which, he then discovered, had been anticipated by Christianity.

Chesterton formulated his own views in opposition to those current at the time, and in a chapter called "The Maniac" attacked the excessive and narrow rationalism of those doctrines of materialism and determinism that were so dear to the age of science and evolution. His point was that logical consistency, however impressive, can just as well be a mark of madness as of sound judgment: a lunatic is "a man who has lost everything except his reason." The man whose reasoning is most superbly consistent, who lets no occurrence escape his logical net, is the paranoiac. Chesterton suggested that the systems of materialistic determinism so fashionable among the scientifically minded had precisely the same quality as the systematic delusions of the madman: seen from inside, they were impressive, consistent, and irrefutable, but seen from outside, preposterously narrow. They were characterized by "the combination of an expansive and exhaustive reason with a contracted common sense. They are universal only in the sense that they take one thin explanation and carry it very far."[8]

* By "orthodoxy," he meant the basics of Christianity contained in the Apostles' Creed.

He believed that this loss of a sense of proportion, this fatal contraction of mental scope, results precisely from the intellectual *hubris* that is determined to fit everything into one clear intellectual pattern. To do justice to experience—for instance, to our experiences of both causation and free will—one must put up with some obscurity and mystery:

Mysticism keeps men sane. As long as you have mystery you have health; when you destroy mystery you create morbidity. The ordinary man has always been sane because the ordinary man has always been a mystic. . . . He has always cared more for truth than for consistency. If he saw two truths that seemed to contradict each other, he would take the two truths and the contradiction along with them.

However, it was no part of Chesterton's purpose to throw away reason and plunge into unlimited mysticism. The next chapter, entitled "The Suicide of Thought," was concerned with what seemed to him the utterly paralyzing relativism of much current thinking: "At any street corner we may meet a man who utters the frantic and blasphemous statement that he may be wrong. . . . We are on the road to producing a race of men too mentally modest to believe in the multiplication table."[9] His particular target was the popular version of evolution with its vague implication that everything, even our standards of true and false, right and wrong, is in a process of perpetual change. As Chesterton pointed out, no one holding such views can *act:* for action demands a certainty about aims and ideals that is dissolved by this notion of evolution. And he went on to indicate some of his own firm ideals. The first of these was democracy:

I was brought up a Liberal, and have always believed in democracy, in the elementary liberal doctrine of a self-governing humanity. If anyone finds the phrase vague or threadbare, I can only pause for a moment to explain that the principle of democracy, as I mean it, can be stated in two propositions. The first is this: that the things common to all men are more important than the things peculiar to any men. . . .
This is the first principle of democracy: that the essential things in men are the things they hold in common, not the things they hold

27

separately. And the second principle is merely this: that the political instinct or desire is one of these things which they hold in common. ... In short, the democratic faith is this: that the most terribly important things must be left to ordinary men themselves—the mating of the sexes, the rearing of the young, the laws of the state. This is democracy; and in this I have always believed.[10]

Chesterton wished, therefore, to make a democratic appeal from the little band of self-selected "experts" to the popular experience of life—which could, he suggested, be found just as well in popular stories or fairy tales as anywhere else. In *Orthodoxy* he used examples from fairy tales to indicate the philosophy of life he had gradually built up for himself; then he described how, having achieved a perplexed vision of existence and its oddities, he discovered that Christianity fitted it so closely that the apparently irrational points in Christianity corresponded to the unintelligible oddities of experience. His aim was to present Christianity as the doctrine of common-sense sanity which corresponds to ordinary human experience. He maintained in typically paradoxical style that it was the atheists Huxley, Herbert Spencer, and Bradlaugh who had converted him to Christianity, simply because their attacks were mutually contradictory. Christianity was attacked because it was too optimistic and because it was too pessimistic; for being violent and for being pacifist; as the enemy of the family and as its defender—and so on. Chesterton describes how he came to a startling conclusion:

Suppose we heard an unknown man spoken of by many men. Suppose we were puzzled to hear that some men said he was too tall and some too short; some objected to his fatness, some lamented his leanness; some thought him too dark, and some too fair. One explanation (as has been already admitted) would be that he might be an odd shape. But there is another explanation. He might be the right shape. Outrageously tall men might feel him to be short. Very short men might feel him to be tall. Old bucks who are growing stout might consider him insufficiently filled out; old beaux who were growing thin might feel that he expanded beyond the narrow lines of elegance.[11]

Not content with presenting Christianity as the viewpoint of the sane man, who is not led astray by partial overemphases, Chesterton took his attack right into the enemies' camp by maintaining—in the face of all the "progressive" thought of his day—that Christianity was also the only firm basis for social reform and revolution:

... reform implies form. It implies that we are trying to shape the world in a particular image; to make it something that we see already in our minds. Evolution is a metaphor from mere automatic unrolling. Progress is a metaphor from merely walking along a road—very likely the wrong road. But reform is a metaphor for reasonable and determined men: it means that we see a certain thing out of shape and we mean to put it into shape. And we know what shape.[12]

Without definite ideals, he asserted, action is paralyzed. The revolutionaries of the eighteenth century had been quite clear about their principles, and had therefore been able to get down to action, whereas the reformers of his own time were rendered helpless by their doubts: "As long as the vision of heaven is always changing, the vision of earth will be exactly the same. No ideal will remain long enough to be realised, or even partly realized. The modern young man will never change his environment; for he will always change his mind."[13] It seemed to Chesterton that Christianity, besides providing the strict rule that the rebel needs if he is to be effective, also provided the only sound basis for democracy; the twin beliefs that all men are made in the image of God (even the poor), and that all men are tainted with Original Sin (even the rich). Furthermore Christianity, with its epic vision of human life as an adventure marked out by the promise of heaven and the danger of hell, seemed to him conducive to heroic political action in a way that no deterministic world view could be. (He had, of course, no experience of the curious and self-contradictory strength that Marxist activists can draw from the belief that Revolution is inevitable.)

Orthodoxy is an extremely vivid and interesting book; the only doubtful question is how orthodox it is. Chesterton demonstrated to his own satisfaction that the fashionable doctrines of materialism, determinism, and evolution made for mental and political paralysis, and that Christianity alone was a sane and liberating doctrine that could enable a man both to believe his experience and to change his environment. But whether Christian authorities were grateful for the demonstration is doubtful. After Chesterton's eventual conversion to Roman Catholicism in 1922, the Church, doubtless glad of so influential a convert, allowed him to pursue his idiosyncratic explanations of doctrine without comment: but the fact remains that Christian traditions are an immense and untidy treasure house from which it is possible to extract support for a great many different philosophical or political positions. Chesterton found much of the Thomist tradition of Catholic thought very congenial indeed, as he later demonstrated in his study of *St. Thomas Aquinas;* but to the complementary Augustinian tradition he was, significantly, antipathetic. That is to say, it is not clear that Chesterton did in fact manage to close the circle of his original paradox, and to arrive at an obvious and traditional truth simply by following his own reflections. As we shall have occasion to notice, a parallel problem arises in his defense of the standpoint of the common man.

All the same, the enterprise of setting out to discover the obvious, though it may be paradoxical, is not nonsensical, as we can see if we turn to Chesterton's literary criticism. Literary criticism—unless it is a matter of learned annotation of texts, and the elucidation of recondite references—is an odd business, for it sets out to tell the reader what he should be able to find out for himself by reading the text. Chesterton's own most notable works of criticism, his books on Browning and Dickens, were reinterpretations justified by his populist stance. In both cases, he claimed that the intentions and virtues of the writers had been misunderstood, because intellectuals had read into them over-intellectual preoccupations. What therefore needed to be reasserted, he thought, was the degree to which they were ordinary men.

This was a particularly paradoxical angle from which to approach Browning, who in that age (when T. S. Eliot was undreamed of) seemed a notoriously "difficult" poet. But Chesterton began by setting this intellectual difficulty in a new perspective:

> ... it is a great deal more difficult to speak finally about his life than about his work. His work has the mystery which belongs to the complex; his life the much greater mystery which belongs to the simple. He was clever enough to understand his own poetry; and if he understood it, we can understand it. But he was also entirely unconscious and impulsive, and he was never clever enough to understand his own character; consequently we may be excused if that part of him which was hidden from him is partly hidden from us. The subtle man is always immeasurably easier to understand than the natural man; for the subtle man keeps a diary of his moods, he practises the art of self-analysis and self-revelation, and can tell us how he came to feel this or to say that. But a man like Browning knows no more about the state of his emotions than about the state of his pulse. ...
>
> This mystery of the unconscious man, far deeper than any mystery of the conscious one, existing as it does in all men, existed peculiarly in Browning, because he was a very ordinary and spontaneous man. The same thing exists to some extent in all history and all affairs. Anything that is deliberate, twisted, created as a trap and a mystery, must be discovered at last; everything that is done naturally remains mysterious. It may be difficult to discover the principles of the Rosicrucians, but it is much easier to discover the principles of the Rosicrucians than the principles of the United States: nor has any secret society kept its aims so quiet as humanity. The way to be inexplicable is to be chaotic, and on the surface this was the quality of Browning's life; there is the same difference between judging of his poetry and judging of his life, that there is between making a map of a labyrinth and making a map of a mist.[14]

Chesterton maintained that where Browning's poems were obscure this came about, not because he was acting the part of the remote intellectual, but because he was himself full of ideas and knowledge, and not sufficiently self-conscious to realize that other people lacked his intellectual equipment. It gave Chesterton unmistakable satisfaction to maintain that Browning was a thoroughly conventional middle-class Victorian, with a conventional hatred of bohemianism. What emerges from the book, in fact, is the claim that this obscure genius was not at all an intellectual aristocrat remote from ordinary concerns, but rather an exaggerated version of Chesterton's ideal common man: conventional, domestic, spontaneous, intensely interested in people, and capable of enjoying life thoroughly.[15]

His version of Dickens, presented on similar lines, has often been praised. He blew a first blast of his populist trumpet with the claim, in the course of a description of the Revolutionary era in which Dickens grew up, that what produces great men is not a belief in supermen, but a belief in equality: the conviction that all men are potential heroes. His analysis of Dickens's achievement and appeal was based on the twin theses that Dickens is supreme because he represents popular literature at its best, and that in his novels ordinary people are displayed in all their magnificence. He claimed that Dickens's novels should not be regarded as attempts at literature in the modern sense, but rather as the culmination of folklore:

Dickens was a mythologist rather than a novelist; he was the last of the mythologists, and perhaps the greatest. He did not always manage to make his characters men, but he always managed, at the least, to make them gods. They are creatures like Punch or Father Christmas. They live statically, in a perpetual summer of being themselves. It was not the aim of Dickens to show the effect of time and circumstance upon a character; it was not even his aim to show the effect of a character on time and circumstance. . . . It was his aim to show character hung in a kind of happy void. . . .

To every man alive, one must hope, it has in some manner happened that he has talked with his more fascinating friends round a table on some night when all the numerous personalities unfolded themselves like great tropical flowers. All fell into their parts as in some delightful impromptu play. Every man was more himself than he had ever been in this vale of tears. Every man was a beautiful caricature of himself. The man who has known such nights will understand the exaggerations of *Pickwick*.[16]

It is illuminating to contrast this with Bernard Shaw's equally characteristic view that Dickens made his characters grotesque caricatures because that is how ordinary human beings appear to the genius![17]

One feature of Dickens's work for which every critic must account is its astonishing popularity, both in Dickens's own time and since. Chesterton remarked that the average literary critic was inclined to regard this popularity as a stumbling block, on the grounds that popular literature is normally bad literature. But Chesterton met the charge head on:

The public does not like bad literature. The public likes a certain kind of literature and likes that kind of literature even when it is bad better than another kind of literature even when it is good. . . .

Dickens stands first as a defiant monument of what happens when a great literary genius has a literary taste akin to that of the community. For this kinship was deep and spiritual. Dickens was not like our ordinary demagogues and journalists. Dickens did not write what the people wanted. Dickens wanted what the people wanted. . . .

His power, then, lay in the fact that he expressed with an energy and brilliancy quite uncommon the things close to the common mind.[18]

Chesterton's triumphant vindication of Dickens as the great democratic genius is one of his most successful enterprises. He does show simultaneously why Dickens is good and why he is popular, and manages to demonstrate something that is obvious when pointed out to us, but not before. We have suggested that this kind of idiosyncratic discovery of the obvious was Chesterton's characteristic strategy, and the reader, having seen him use this method to arrive at popular taste, common sense, and orthodox religion, might suppose that such a naturally conservative procedure should lead him to a political standpoint akin to Burke's. Here, however, as in the case of Chesterton's reinterpretation of religious orthodoxy, we run up against the kaleidoscopic quality of ideas, their capacity for endless rearrangement: for of course Chesterton's political standpoint was the reverse of Burkean. In his hands, common sense became the sense of the common man, asserted against his aristocratic and intellectual mentors, and orthodox religion became the guardian of the revolutionary tradition. Indeed, in one of his moments of paradoxical exaggeration he went so far as to maintain that, in the great debate over the French Revolution, Burke stood for atheism and Robespierre for faith in God—on the grounds that Robespierre appealed to eternal justice and the universal rights of man, whereas Burke replied with the insidiously relativistic doctrines of historical evolution and the rights of Englishmen.[19]

Chesterton's intellectual ancestor from that revolutionary period was not Burke but William Cobbett, of whom he wrote an excellent study. The two men had a great deal in common, not least the fact that their political views tended to be misunderstood and misrepresented because they eluded political labels. Chesterton was variously regarded as a Tory and a Radical, while Cobbett passed in party terms from extreme Toryism to flaming radicalism, and was never at ease with his fellow partisans in either camp. Chesterton shared Cobbett's ideal of the independent farmer secure on his own land, and his hatred alike of aristocratic government and industrial society.

Above all, the point of kinship that Chesterton felt most strongly was the paradoxical ability to see obvious things—or rather, things that would be obvious, but for the mystifying power of clichés. Again and again in his book on Cobbett, he stressed this point:

William Cobbett was pre-eminently a man with eyes in his head. . . .

He could see before he could read. Most modern people can read before they can see. They have read about a hundred things long before they have seen one of them. Most town children have read about corn or cattle as if they were dwarfs or dragons, long before they have seen a grain of wheat or a cow. Many of them have read about ships or churches, or the marching of soldiers or the crowd cheering a king, or any other normal sight, which they have never seen. By a weird mesmerism which it is not here necessary to analyse, what people read has a sort of magic power over their sight. It lays a spell on their eyes, so that they see what they expect to see. They do not see the most solid and striking things that contradict what they expect to see. . . . Cobbett was a man without these magic spectacles.[20]

As a result, said Chesterton, Cobbett was able to see clearly the condition to which the English poor had been reduced by "improving" landlords, and to detect the growing evils of "progress" in industry. He could even see the evidence that contradicted the Whig interpretation of English history. For there, standing up in the English landscape—contradicting the accepted thesis of progress from the barbarous, tyrannical, and priest-ridden Middle Ages to the enlightened and liberal modern world—were on the one hand the magnificent Gothic parish church which the men of the Middle Ages had built for their whole community, and on the other the ruinous cottages of the poor, at a proper distance from the vast eighteenth-century mansion of the landlord.

Chesterton—as usual, reading into his subject a great many of his own opinions—admired Cobbett for his ability to see through the clichés of his age to the power structure that they concealed, and for his courage in shouting aloud what he had discovered. Similarly, he stressed the directness of Cobbett's sympathy with the sufferings of the poor. He illustrated this by referring to a passage in Cobbett's *Rural Rides:*

He describes . . . how he started out riding with his son at dawn; how some hitch occurred about the inn at which he had intended to breakfast, and he rode on hoping to reach another hostelry in reasonable time; how other hitches occurred which annoyed him, making him scold the boy for some small blunders about the strapping of a bag; and how he awoke at last to a sort of wonder as to why he should be so irritable with a child he loved so much. And then it dawned upon him that it was for the very simple reason that he had had no breakfast. He, who had fed well the night before and intended to feed well again, who was well clothed and well mounted, could not deny that a good appetite might gradually turn into a bad temper. And then, with one of his dramatic turns or gestures, he suddenly summons up before us all the army of Englishmen who had no hope of having any breakfast until they could somehow beg work from hard or indifferent men; who wandered about the world in a normal state of hunger and anger and blank despair about the future; who were exposed to every insult and impotent under every wrong; and who were expected by the politicians and the papers to be perfectly mild and moderate in their language, perfectly loyal and law-abiding in their sentiments, to invoke blessings on all who were more fortunate and respectfully touch their hats to anybody who had a little more money.[21]

As Chesterton said, the point of Cobbett's method is that it makes the reader understand poverty from the inside: "He knows for the first time what is meant by saying that men are brothers, and not merely poor relations. That is the psychological experience corresponding to the philosophical doctrine which for many remains a mystery: the equality of man."[22]

This book on Cobbett brings out clearly the connections between Chesterton's politics, his philosophy of life, and even his very style. His purpose was above all to pierce through the clichés that cloud experience, and to make his readers see things as they are: and the most important thing this vision could reveal to them was the reality, and the supreme importance, of other people—especially those whom the influential tend to forget (like the chauffeur in *The Flying Inn* who is faint with hunger because his employer, fully engaged in being sensitive and humanitarian, has never stopped to arrange a meal for him). As he constantly stressed, the very phrases that the literate use tend to cloud the reality of human experience: "if we want to talk about poverty, we must talk about it as the hunger of a human being. . . . We must say first of the beggar, not that there is insufficient housing accommodation, but that he has not where to lay his head."[23]

Comparison with Cobbett brings out one rather curious feature of Chesterton's position: unlike Cobbett, he certainly could not "see before he could read." He was not a man of the people, but a scion of the upper middle class. He was not a country child, but a Londoner, born and bred. He had been an exceptionally bookish, dreamy child, and was to be famous for absent-minded impracticality as a man. In other words, Chesterton belongs to the not altogether rare category of the *reformed* intellectual, whose views about his former vices are often as severe as those of the reformed drunkard.

It is common enough, in the history of ideas, for writers to lay stress precisely upon the perceptions that they have seen as blinding revelations, and on the virtues that do not come naturally to them. Rousseau is perhaps the most striking example —the intellectual who turned his back on philosophy, the social climber who left the Parisian salons for the simple life, the inveterate sinner turned moralist—but the phenomenon is common enough and perfectly intelligible. As an adolescent, Chesterton had gone through a period of deep depression, compounded of solipsistic fears that the world was illusion, and horrifying fantasies of evil. When he emerged from this into maturity, his philosophy was a triumphant reaction against his own experience. After fearing that the cosmos might be only a dream, he laid great stress on the vividness and value of ordinary things. After covering his notebooks with evil faces and instruments of torture, he became the kindest of men, deeply attentive to the feelings of others. After being sunk in depression, he became a prophet of the joy and excitement of everyday life. Despite all his praise of other writers—Cobbett, Browning, Dickens—for their direct and simple response to life, Chesterson was himself one of the twice-born, his own innocence and spontaneity something gratefully recovered from this youthful crisis.

Once he had emerged from the neurotic imaginings of adolescence into what he thankfully recognized as the daylight of sanity, Chesterton set out to convert his generation from the intellectual fads clouding their minds. In particular, he believed that the social and political doctrines of conservatives and reformers alike ignored the realities of human nature. From the politicians and social theorists on both sides, he appealed to the people. But as is commonly the case with populists, his picture of the needs and desires of the common man—and especially of the common woman—was idiosyncratic and selective; we must now examine it in more detail.

3

Beer and Liberty
versus Soap and Socialism

1. Social Reform and the Rights of the Poor

HISTORY OF HUDGE AND GUDGE

There is, let us say, a certain filthy rookery in Hoxton, dripping with disease and honeycombed with crime and promiscuity. There are, let us say, two noble and courageous young men, of pure intentions and (if you prefer it) noble birth; let us call them Hudge and Gudge. Hudge, let us say, is of a bustling sort; he points out that the people must at all costs be got out of this den; he subscribes and collects money, but he finds (despite the large financial interests of the Hudges) that the thing will have to be done on the cheap if it is to be done on the spot. He therefore runs up a row of tall bare tenements like beehives; and soon has all the poor people bundled into their little brick cells, which are certainly better than their old quarters, in so far as they are weather proof, well ventilated and supplied with clean water. But Gudge has a more delicate nature. He feels a nameless something lacking in the little brick boxes; he raises numberless objections; he even assails the celebrated Hudge Report, with the Gudge Minority Report; and by the end of a year or so has come to telling Hudge heatedly that the people were much happier where they were before. As the people preserve in both places precisely the same air of dazed amiability, it is very difficult to find out which is right. But at least one might safely say that no people ever liked stench or star-

39

vation as such, but only some peculiar pleasures entangled with them. Not so feels the sensitive Gudge. Long before the final quarrel (Hudge *v.* Gudge and Another), Gudge has succeeded in persuading himself that slums and stinks are really very nice things; that the habit of sleeping fourteen in a room is what has made our England great; and that the smell of open drains is absolutely necessary to the rearing of a viking breed.

But meanwhile, has there been no degeneration in Hudge? Alas, I fear there has. Those maniacally ugly buildings which he originally put up as unpretentious sheds barely to shelter human life, grow every day more and more lovely to his deluded eye. Things he would never have dreamed of defending, except as crude necessities, things like common kitchens or infamous asbestos stoves, begin to shine quite sacredly before him, merely because they reflect the wrath of Gudge. He maintains, with the aid of eager little books by Socialists, that man is really happier in a hive than in a house. The practical difficulty of keeping total strangers out of your bedroom he describes as Brotherhood; and the necessity for climbing twenty-three flights of cold stone stairs, I dare say he calls Effort. The net result of their philanthropic adventure is this; that one has come to defending indefensible slums and still more indefensible slum-landlords; while the other has come to treating as divine the sheds and pipes which he only meant as desperate. Gudge is now a corrupt and apoplectic old Tory in the Carlton Club; if you mention poverty to him he roars at you in a thick, hoarse voice something that is conjectured to be "Do 'em good." Nor is Hudge more happy; for he is a lean vegetarian with a grey, pointed beard and an unnaturally easy smile, who goes about telling everybody that at last we shall all sleep in one universal bedroom; and he lives in a Garden City, like one forgotten of God.

Such is the lamentable history of Hudge and Gudge; which I merely introduce as a type of an endless and exasperating misunderstanding which is always occurring in modern England. To get men out of a rookery men are put into a tenement; and at the beginning the healthy human soul loathes them both. A man's first desire is to get away as far as possible from the rookery, even should his mad course lead him to a model dwelling. The second desire is, naturally, to get away from the model dwelling, even if it should lead a man back to the rookery. But I am neither a Hudgian nor a Gudgian; and I think the mistakes of these two famous and fascinating persons arose from one single fact. They arose from the fact that neither Hudge nor Gudge had ever thought for an instant what sort of house a man might probably like for himself. In short, they did not begin with the ideal; and, therefore, were not practical politicians.[1]

One of the reviewers of *What's Wrong with the World,* in which this passage appears, asked in bewilderment whether Chesterton was a Conservative or a Radical.[2] It is easy to understand his confusion, for at the same time that Chesterton attacked the rich and their exploitation of the poor, he also opposed all the current attempts at social reform, whether Socialist or Liberal. Chesterton himself maintained that he was simply a Liberal, still fighting for principles that the party had deserted. In a speech entitled, "Why I am Not an Official Liberal,"[3] he once declared, "I am a Liberal. It is the other people who are not Liberals." There is a lot more to be said for this claim than one might expect.

The Edwardian age in Britain is generally regarded as a great age of social reform, the time when the foundations of the welfare state were laid. Education of children had been compulsory since 1880, but in 1906 local authorities were empowered to provide free school meals where necessary, and in 1907 compulsory medical inspection of school children was introduced. In 1908 old age pensions were introduced for people over seventy. Above all, in 1911 the Liberal government instituted contributory national health insurance for all wage earners, along with unemployment insurance for men in certain trades. All this legislation showed not only a new preoccupation with the welfare of the poor, but also an increasing conviction, among Liberals and Tories as well as Socialists, that social welfare was a national responsibility, and could not be left to private charity.[4] The work of social investigators like Booth and Rowntree had demonstrated beyond any shadow of doubt that poverty and

41

destitution were not merely an accidental condition into which the idle and improvident might fall, but the normal state of at least a third of the whole population.[5]

Meanwhile, horror at such revelations was taken out of the realm of soft-hearted philanthropy and into that of hard-headed imperial politics by worries about Britain's international position. The unchallenged industrial supremacy enjoyed by Britain in the mid-nineteenth century was increasingly threatened, especially by Germany; while the news that forty per cent of the men recruited by the army during the Boer War had been rejected as unfit[6] brought home the point that poverty in Britain was not compatible with greatness abroad. As Lord Roseberry put it in an egregious speech:

An Empire such as ours requires as its first condition an imperial race—a race vigorous and industrious and intrepid. . . . In the rookeries and slums which still survive, an imperial race cannot be reared. . . . Remember that where you promote health and arrest disease, where you convert an unhealthy citizen into a healthy one . . . you in doing your duty are also working for the Empire.[7]

The authorities were sufficiently disturbed to appoint an Inter-Departmental Committee on Physical Deterioration, and it was in the light of this committee's representations that free school meals were instituted in 1906 and compulsory medical inspection in 1907. Fear of competition from Germany was accompanied by admiration of her policies for national efficiency, and many of the welfare reforms of the period were directly modeled on German institutions.

It would be naive to regard the Liberal welfare reforms as the outcome of pure philanthropy. What it is more important to appreciate, however, if we are to understand Chesterton's opposition to these measures, is the consistently paternalistic and repressive attitude of the philanthropic reformers, whether Liberal, Conservative, or Socialist. From the traditionalists of the Charity Organization Society, an authoritarian brand of philanthropy was only to be expected; perhaps the same could be said of the Socialists, chiefly represented in elite circles by the Fabian Society, whose aim was state control and organization of all resources. Liberals generally criticized Socialists on the grounds that their policies would mean the end not only of property but of liberty, and the regimentation of society by bureaucrats modeled on the formidable Mrs. Webb. However, the records of the period make it clear that there was singularly little difference between Fabian Socialists and Liberals, where treatment of the poor was concerned. The two might differ on the issues of state control of property, and the liberties of property owners, but there was an astonishing unspoken consensus between them that the poor had no right to liberty, and that bureaucratic regulation was perfectly acceptable when applied to them.

One clear illustration of this point can be found in the popularity of a favorite social remedy of the period: the notion of dealing with the unemployed by putting them into labor colonies.[8] It was generally accepted that, if this policy were pursued, the deserving poor must be separated from the idle loafers, and the latter put under some kind of reformatory discipline. Beatrice Webb spent much time and thought upon this group, and suggested at one point that "compulsory technical training or military or other training . . . absorbing the whole time of the man from 6 A.M. to 10 P.M." might be best.[9] What is notable, however, is the prospect that was held out to those who were *not* officially regarded as loafers, but who were recognized as being unemployed through no fault of their own. The most canvassed suggestion was that they should be employed in labor colonies in the countryside away from their wives and children. In other words, the men were to live in barracks, under discipline and separate from their families, just as if they were prisoners or soldiers.

The remarkable feature of such schemes is the unanimity with which they were put forward, not only by Socialists like Beatrice

Webb, or by authoritarian philanthropists like the leaders of the Salvation Army, but also by Liberals. There is a revealing article by Charles Masterman, a Liberal friend of Chesterton's and afterward a member of Asquith's Liberal reforming government, in a book to which Chesterton also contributed.[10] Masterman recommended

the double system of labour colonies for those who desire work in temporary unemployment, acceptable by free men, carrying none of the degradations of charity and State relief, and of penal colonies for those who do not desire work, as humane as may be, but deliberately designed for the elimination of the "loafer" and the "cadger."[11]

Tactful phrasing cannot alter the substance of the proposal, with its double affront to the liberty of the poor: in the first place their classification—inevitably, on the basis of a personal inquisition—as "deserving" or "undeserving"; and in the second place the loss, even by the admittedly deserving, of their liberty. Concern to make sure that only the deserving benefited from welfare schemes was in fact a leitmotif of all the Liberal legislation of the period. Old age pensions, for instance, introduced in 1908 for those over seventy, were withheld from those who had been in prison or who had "persistently failed to work." This concern was most conspicuous in the administration of the National Insurance Act, since it was inconsistent with the contributory principle of the Act. Under the Act certain trades were liable to compulsory contributions for unemployment insurance; having contributed, a workman might reasonably have expected that he had an automatic right to relief if out of work. Not so, however: he was in fact excluded from benefit if he had been discharged for misconduct—"insolence," for example—or if he had given up his job "without just cause." In the first two years of the Act's operation, over 50,000 claims for benefit were disallowed on such grounds.[12]

It is clear, in fact, that no notion ever crossed the minds of most of those concerned with the poor, that the poor themselves might have any rights to personal liberty or privacy. In this sense the new social reforms simply carried on the old tradition of the Poor Law, under which the price of charity had been entry into the workhouse, which involved loss of one's liberty, separation from one's family, and a degradation in the eyes of society symbolized by loss of the right to vote. Charles Booth, the great social investigator and philanthropist, put the matter succinctly in his book, *Life and Labour of the People of London:*

... what I have to propose may be considered as an extension of the Poor Law. What is the Poor Law system? It is a limited form of Socialism—a Socialistic community (aided from outside) living in the midst of an Individualist nation. . . . My idea is to make the dual system, Socialism in the arms of Individualism, under which we already live, more efficient by extending somewhat the sphere of the former and making the division of function more distinct. Our Individualism fails because our Socialism is incomplete. In taking charge of the lives of the incapable, State Socialism finds its proper work, and by doing it completely, would relieve us of a serious danger. . . . Thorough interference on the part of the State with the lives of a small fraction of the population would tend to make it possible, ultimately, to dispense with any Socialistic interference in the lives of all the rest.[13]

To a modern reader, the most conspicuous feature of Edwardian discussions on social policy is the assumed gulf between rich and poor. The working classes were a problem, an object of pity or of legislation; but it occurred to scarcely any of the reformers to regard them as people, in the sense in which he would regard ladies and gentlemen as people. The tone is that of organized compassion for an inferior race of beings. The R.S.-P.C.A. and the Anti-Vivisection League never thought it necessary to consult the wishes of the creatures they attempted to rescue, and neither did the social reformers.

It was in this setting that Chesterton found himself maintaining what seemed to him the traditional principles of liberalism, in opposition to almost all the self-styled Liberals. For the main difference between Chesterton and the welfare reformers was his vivid sense of common humanity with the poor: his conviction that, physically and spiritually, the poor were just the same as the rich, and that they too desired not regimentation but the right to live their own lives with their own families in security and privacy. The essence of his position was that the rights which the upper and middle classes had gained for themselves should be rights for the poor as well. His generation was coming to realize that poverty and unemployment were often in no sense a man's own fault, but imposed upon him by circumstances outside his control; but instead of altering these conditions the reformers, Liberal and Socialist alike, added to the injury of exploitation the insult of regimentation. Chesterton's view was that this cure was as bad as the disease, and that justice demanded the redistribution of property, to enable the poor to live in freedom and independence like the rich.

Chesterton himself was of course a member of the middle class, in no way representative of the poor. As he pointed out during a controversy with Bernard Shaw and H. G. Wells, *none* of the self-appointed reformers actually knew the poor and their feelings from the inside. However, the principle upon which he took his stand was that human nature, human needs, and human feelings are universal, and that the security, domesticity, and privacy which the majority in the middle classes valued so highly for themselves, were also what the poor would want if anyone were to give them the choice.[14]

Chesterton was a fighter by nature: he loved nothing better than controversy. And one of the most important things to grasp, in trying to understand his position, is that he was generally fighting on at least three fronts at once. In the first place, he fought alongside all the humanitarian idealists of his generation against defenders of a society in which one third of the population was perpetually on the verge of starvation, while millionaires and aristocrats lived in luxury. Thus far, his position was perfectly straightforward. However, Chesterton fought not only against the rich and their admirers, but also—simultaneously—against two distinct segments of the humanitarian idealists themselves: the Liberals and the Socialists.

He fought against the Liberal advocates of social welfare because, while they knew the value of liberty and property for themselves and their own families, they were prepared—on the best philanthropic grounds—to regiment the poor. The movement for prohibition of the sale of alcohol in Britain and America seemed to him the classic case of this, and his simplest argument against it was that it implied one law for the poor and another for the rich. "The recent reform which restricted intoxicants to the wealthier classes," was his sardonic description of Prohibition in America.[15] Virtually all Liberal social legislation seemed to him to involve such a blatant double standard.

So at the same time that he fought against social injustice, Chesterton also denounced the social reforms by which the upper classes were imposing restrictions and regulations on the lower that they would never have accepted for themselves. To this extent, he was on the side of those Socialists who regarded welfare legislation merely as a way of shoring up the capitalist system.* However, this was the only common ground he had with the Socialists. With some of them indeed—notably Bernard Shaw—he was on very friendly terms throughout his life. But he never ceased to maintain that the Socialist ideal was fundamentally mistaken, and that, while a utopia in which all private property were abolished would certainly be less unjust than the existing arrangement, regimentation for everyone was no more desirable than regimentation for the poor.

This habit of launching controversial attacks in three directions at once could well give rise to confusion, as he himself realized. All the more reason, then, to make clear not only what he was against, but what he was for. He set out to do this in *What's Wrong with the World,* published in 1910.

---

* The only radical MPs who opposed the National Insurance Act were six left-wing Labour members, who objected to the contributory principle. The bulk of the Labour Party supported the Act.

What's Wrong with the World is vintage Chesterton, full of the sparkling energy characteristic of his best work, immensely readable and pre-eminently quotable. Like all his most successful writing, it conveys a subtle and coherent point of view expressed in a deceptively simple and casual manner, apparently rambling through entertaining digressions. It is interesting to compare Chesterton's style with Belloc's, for although the two were friends and shared a good many opinions, the tone of their thought is quite different. Belloc's controversial writing—for instance, in *The Servile State*—is a tour de force of brilliant organization, with all his arguments marshaled into a clear logical structure that can be readily summarized and expounded. Chesterton's writings, on the contrary, resist summary and demand quotation: for the impression they create is less that of an argument, logically developed and open to logical refutation, than of a way of seeing humanity and showing it to others. The parables, the jokes, and the paradoxes play an essential part in this, and are not merely frivolities decorating an essentially independent argument. Much of our account of *What's Wrong with the World* will therefore be in Chesterton's own words.

One of Chesterton's favorite paradoxes was that there is nothing so necessary to practical action as an abstract ideal, and *What's Wrong* begins with a version of this point. He remarks that "it is the whole definition and dignity of man that in social matters we must actually find the cure before we find the disease." The medical analogies so frequently applied to the condition of society lead us astray here: for while all doctors are agreed about their aim, the restoration of the normal healthy body, in social matters the difficulty is that "some men are aiming at cures which other men would regard as worse maladies: are offering ultimate conditions as states of health which others would uncompromisingly call states of disease."[16]

The situation would not be hopeless if people were at least clear about their conflicting ideals: but what Chesterton particularly deplored was an increasing unwillingness to specify ends, a tendency to call for a vague "efficiency" and an undefined "progress." He insisted that there was no virtue in going forward as such, and that in some respects men would do much better to go back to older ideals and institutions.

We often read nowadays of the valour or audacity with which some rebel attacks a hoary tyranny or an antiquated superstition. There is not really any courage at all in attacking hoary or antiquated things, any more than in offering to fight one's grandmother. The really courageous man is he who defies tyrannies young as the morning and superstitions fresh as the first flowers. The only true free-thinker is he whose intellect is as much free from the future as from the past. He cares as little for what will be as for what has been; he cares only for what ought to be.[17]

His own social ideal was nothing new, but ancient—domesticity: a man, his wife, and his children living in their own home in safety. This, as Chesterton knew, was an ideal that seemed utterly boring, restrictive, and outdated to the progressive intellectuals of his time. Unlike them, however, he saw the home as the sphere of liberty for the ordinary mass of mankind. For instance, it offered them their only chance of personal expression and artistic creativity.

For the mass of men the idea of artistic creation can only be expressed by an idea unpopular in present discussions—the idea of property. The average man cannot cut clay into the shape of a man; but he can cut earth into the shape of a garden; and though he arranges it with red geraniums and blue potatoes in alternate straight lines, he is still an artist; because he has chosen. The average man cannot paint the sunset whose colours he admires; but he can paint his own house with what colour he chooses; and though he paints it pea green with pink spots, he is still an artist; because that is his choice. Property is merely the art of the democracy. It means that every man should have something that he can shape in his own image as he is shaped in the image of Heaven.[18]

According to Chesterton, the fashionable boredom with domestic life was a feature of excessive riches, and quite irrelevant to the experience of ordinary men and women:

... of all the modern notions generated by mere wealth the worst is this: the notion that domesticity is dull and tame. Inside the house (they say) is dead decorum and routine; outside is adventure and variety. This is indeed a rich man's opinion. The rich man knows that his own house moves on vast and soundless wheels of wealth: is run by regiments of servants, by a swift and silent ritual. On the other hand, every sort of vagabondage or romance is open to him in the streets outside. He has plenty of money and can afford to be a tramp. His wildest adventure will end in a restaurant, while the yokel's tamest adventure may end in a police-court. If he smashes a window he can pay for it; if he smashes a man he can pension him. . . . And because he, the luxurious man, dictates the tone of nearly all "advanced" and "progressive" thought, we have almost forgotten what a home really means to the overwhelming millions of mankind.

For the truth is, that to the moderately poor the home is the only place of liberty.[19]

What the ordinary, average man wants, then, is a wife, children, and a house of his own—*not* a flat or even a semi-detached, but a house of his own: "He does not merely want a roof above him and a chair below him; he wants an objective and visible kingdom; a fire at which he can cook what food he likes, a door he can open to what friends he chooses."[20] However, although Chesterton maintained that virtually every Englishman would have liked a house of his own, he recognized that the poor Englishman of his time stood very little chance of getting one. It was at this point that he introduced the "History of Hudge and Gudge," with which this chapter began, in order to make his point that current controversies between social reformers and Conservatives were tragically irrelevant to the real needs and desires of the English people. Houses they might want, but Tory slums or Socialist model dwellings were all they were likely to get; meanwhile they were even being mystified by the upper classes into believing that this must really be what they wanted.

Under the pressure of certain upper class philosophies (or, in other words, under the pressure of Hudge and Gudge) the average man has really become quite bewildered about the goal of his efforts;

and his efforts, therefore, grow feebler and feebler. His simple notion of having a home of his own is derided as bourgeois, as sentimental or as despicably Christian. . . . Hudge and Gudge, or the governing class generally, will never fail for lack of some modern phrase to cover their ancient predominance. The great lords will refuse the English peasant his three acres and a cow on advanced grounds, if they cannot refuse it any longer on reactionary grounds. They will deny him the three acres on grounds of State Ownership. They will forbid him the cow on grounds of humanitarianism.[21]

In other words, Chesterton was convinced that the reason why the people of England were homeless was that they were ruled by an oligarchy. The vast wealth of these families seemed to Chesterton a travesty of the idea of property: "It is the negation of property that the Duke of Sutherland should have all the farms in one estate; just as it would be the negation of marriage if he had all our wives in one harem."[22] Nevertheless, in spite of this plutocratic distortion, "the idea of private property universal but private, the idea of families free but still families, of domesticity democratic but still domestic, of one man one house—this remains the real vision and magnet of mankind."[23]

In this first part of *What's Wrong with the World*, entitled "The Homelessness of Man," Chesterton had identified what seemed to him the ordinary human ideal of a free family in a safe home, and then the basic evil of his time: the lower classes, after being herded into slums by the rich, were now being herded into workhouses or model dwellings by the reformers. He claimed, in fact, that what human nature demanded was property, but property for *all*, and that by this standard of human needs, both the society of his time and the schemes of most reformers stood condemned. He went on in Part II to elaborate his view of human nature, and to test against it the trends of his time. In this section he was concerned particularly with the nature of man as opposed to woman, since he was a firm believer in far-reaching differences of character between the sexes. In particular he believed that men, unlike women, tended naturally to a kind of comradeship that was democratic in its essence, and that formed the existential basis of republican politics: "There are only three things in the world that women do not understand; and they are Liberty, Equality and Fraternity."[24]

Comradeship involves the recognition that we are all in the same boat, the willingness to treat other men as equals in a somewhat impersonal way—a masculine camaraderie that seemed to Chesterton to be the root of democracy.

Democracy in its human sense is not arbitrament by the majority; it is not even arbitrament by everybody. It can be more nearly defined as arbitrament by anybody. I mean that it rests on that club habit of taking a total stranger for granted, of assuming certain things to be inevitably common to yourself and him. Only the things that anybody may be presumed to hold have the full authority of democracy.[25]

Such democracy was epitomized for him by the society of the English public house, which he defended so passionately against Liberal temperance reformers.

An essential aspect of this natural republicanism, according to Chesterton, was the masculine passion for impersonal rules and formalities.

Men in their aspect of equality and debate adore the idea of rules; they develop and complicate them greatly to excess. A man finds far more regulations and definitions in his club, where there are rules, than in his home, where there is a ruler. A deliberative assembly, the House of Commons, for instance, carries this mummery to the point of a methodical madness. . . . These are, perhaps, fantasies of decay: but fundamentally they answer a masculine appetite. Men feel that rules, even if irrational, are universal; men feel that law is equal, even when it is not equitable.[26]

The complement of this formal and leisurely democracy was the discipline which the most democratic communities can accept in an emergency: for Chesterton emphasized that the obvious necessity of commanders in battle, or in similar straits, had nothing to do with superiority or the existence of supermen, but simply with *urgency*. To explain the English aristocracy, there was no need for fantasies about natural hierarchy or the survival of the fittest: "It is simply an army without an enemy—billeted upon the people."[27]

The really dangerous contemporary threat to man's natural instinct for democracy, Chesterton saw as industrialization. He said in Rousseauian tones, "Democracy has one real enemy, and that is civilization."[28] For modern business requires specialization, hierarchy, and a constant struggle for survival. This mesmerizing process of commercial and industrial expansion for its own sake, directed by "captains of industry" chosen for their ruthlessness, Chesterton chose to label "Imperialism." He admitted that his terminology might cause some confusion, and hastened to distinguish the domination of business from the ordinary Englishman's sentimental attachment to a dimly imagined Empire:

The reasons for believing in Australia are mostly as sentimental as the most sentimental reasons for believing in heaven. New South Wales is quite literally regarded as a place where the wicked cease from troubling and the weary are at rest; that is, a paradise for uncles who have turned dishonest and for nephews who are born tired.[29]

This sentimentalism was a very different matter from what Chesterton himself meant by imperialism: domination by the interests and values of big business, which had drawn England into the Boer War, and which was also drawing more and more people into poverty and unemployment in the London slums. Chesterton denounced this as a monstrous inversion of values:

Our specialised trades in their highly civilised state cannot (it says) be run without the whole brutal business of bossing and sacking, "too old at forty" and all the rest of the filth. . . .

Now (to reiterate my title) this is what is wrong. This is the huge modern heresy of altering the human soul to fit its conditions, instead of altering human conditions to fit the human soul. If soap-boiling is really inconsistent with brotherhood, so much the worse for soap-boiling, not for brotherhood. If civilisation really cannot get on with democracy, so much the worse for civilisation, not for democracy.[30]

Having set against the commercial civilization of his time the ideal of a home for all and democracy among men, Chesterton proceeded in the next section of his book to look at "Feminism: or the Mistake about Woman." This is likely to seem the least persuasive aspect of Chesterton's thought to readers now, but some of his points are still arresting. Chesterton was, and remained, antifeminist. His simplest objection to giving women the vote was that, at the time when he was writing, most of them showed no sign of wanting it. This did not surprise him, however, since he thought that women differed fundamentally from men in their nature and political tendencies. His defense of keeping women in the home was more eloquent than most such arguments, simply because the home seemed to him a very exciting place. He pointed out that housewives and mothers are almost alone in being able to avoid the narrow specialization that is one of the special curses of modern civilization. This was particularly the case where looking after children was concerned: "Babies need not to be taught a trade, but to be introduced to a world. To put the matter shortly, woman is generally shut up in a house with a human being at the time when he asks all the questions that there are, and some that there aren't. It would be odd if she retained any of the narrowness of a specialist."[31]

He agreed that domestic life was very hard work, but emphatically denied that it could be called either dull or trivial: "How can it be a large career to tell other people's children about the Rule of Three, and a small career to tell one's own children about the universe? . . . a woman's function is laborious, but because it is gigantic, not because it is minute. I will pity Mrs. Jones for the hugeness of her task; I will never pity her for its smallness."[32] However, while admiring and in some ways envying the lot of the housewife, Chesterton regarded feminine life as a poor training for politics. Not, be it noted, on intellectual or educational grounds—Chesterton never for a moment admitted that the intellectual or cultured had a right to rule the rest. His claim was rather that women were unable to understand or participate in the comradeship upon which all democracy and impersonal justice was built, and that their own inclination naturally led them toward a kind of impatient despotism.

Chesterton was opposed not only to women's suffrage, but to the whole modern involvement of women in work outside the home, which seemed to him the reverse of liberation. As he put it memorably in another place; "twenty million young women rose to their feet with the cry *We will not be dictated to:* and proceeded to become stenographers."[33] His position in *What's Wrong* is striking, for he argues that women should be kept out of business because they are too conscientious: "Modern women defend their office with all the fierceness of domesticity. They fight for desk and typewriter as for hearth and home, and develop a sort of wolfish wifehood on behalf of the invisible head of the firm. That is why they do office work so well; and that is why they ought not to do it."[34] Woman's emancipation, in other words, seemed to him merely a convenient cover for her exploitation.

The next section of *What's Wrong with the World* is entitled "Education: or, the Mistake about the Child." Chesterton's central point about education was that, to be effective, it must have a definite purpose. Progressive thinkers in his time, as in ours, believed that a better society could be created by means of education and particularly by means of an education that was not authoritarian. Chesterton answered: "The fashionable fallacy is that by education we can give people something that we have not got. . . . These pages have, of course, no other general purpose than to point out that we cannot create anything good until we have conceived it."[35] The worst aspect of this experimental education, from Chesterton's point of view, was that it was chiefly directed at the children of the poor. Education ought to be the passing on by ordinary people to their children of those things that they are most certain of. But:

The trouble in too many of our modern schools is that the State, being controlled so specially by the few, allows cranks and experiments to go straight to the school-room. . . . Obviously, it ought to be the oldest things that are taught to the youngest people; the assured and experienced truths that are put first to the baby. But in a school today the baby has to submit to a system that is younger than himself. . . . But this, as I say, is all due to the mere fact that we are managed by a little oligarchy; my system presupposes that men who govern themselves will govern their children. Today we all use Popular Education as meaning education of the people. I wish I could use it as meaning education by the people.[36]

Chesterton contrasted the state schools to which poor children were compelled to go with the so-called public schools at which the upper classes were educated, and pointed out that—within its narrow limits—the education of the rich was successful, whereas that of the poor was not. The superior effectiveness of Eton and Harrow he attributed to the fact that teachers at public schools really did represent the parents: "The vague politics of the squire, the vaguer virtues of the colonel, the soul and spiritual virtues of a tea merchant are, in veritable practice, conveyed to the children of these people at the English public schools."[37]

The education of the poor, by contrast, was explicitly directed *against* the views and attitudes of the parents. It was to a large extent simply an attempt to imitate public school education in grotesquely inappropriate circumstances. Hence the ludicrous overemphasis on cleanliness and sport. Consequently the particular traditions of the poor were not reinforced in schools, but rather counteracted. Chesterton was thinking here of such things as "that system of prompt and patchwork generosity which is a daily glory of the poor"; the humor of the slums; the great rituals of death and bereavement preserved among the poor. Compulsory education—imposed, of course, only upon the poor—meant taking children out of their homes in order to teach them to despise everything that their parents thought and felt.

I do not expect the pathetic, eager *pietas* of the mother, with her funeral clothes and funeral baked meats, to be exactly imitated in the educational system; but has it any influence at all on the educational system? Does any elementary schoolmaster accord it even an instant's consideration or respect? I do not expect the schoolmaster to hate hospitals and C.O.S.* centres so much as the schoolboy's father; but does he hate them at all? Does he sympathise in the least with the poor man's point of honour against official institutions? Is it not quite certain that the ordinary elementary schoolmaster will think it not merely natural but simply conscientious to eradicate all these rugged legends of a laborious people, and on principle to preach soap and Socialism against beer and liberty? In the lower classes the schoolmaster does not work for the parent but against the parent. Modern education means handing down the customs of the minority, and rooting out the customs of the majority.[38]

The final section of the book, "The Home of Man," summed up Chesterton's claim that the last remnants of liberty were being stolen from poor Englishmen. While on the one hand Tory millionaires ground them down into poverty, on the other hand Socialists were all too willing to cry that property and family life were bourgeois and ought to be abolished. Chesterton insisted that all most people wanted was a house and family life, but that "the overwhelming mass of the English people . . . are simply too poor to be domestic."[39] Domesticity, he thought, could be saved only by a massive redistribution of property—against which, he ventured to suspect, the millionaires and the social reformers were in unholy alliance. He summed up his fight on behalf of the poor against both the rich and the reformers with a story about one of the many cases in which the rights of the poor were being violated on the irreproachable grounds of public health:

A little while ago certain doctors and other persons permitted by modern law to dictate to their shabbier fellow-citizens, sent out an order that all little girls should have their hair cut short. I mean, of course, all little girls whose parents were poor. Many very unhealthy habits are common among rich little girls, but it will be long before any doctors interfere forcibly with them. Now, the case for this particular interference was this, that the poor are pressed down from above into such stinking and suffocating underworlds of squalor, that

* The Charity Organisation Society, an extremely active philanthropic organisation, noted for its paternalism.

poor people must not be allowed to have hair, because in their case it must mean lice in the hair.[40]

The use Chesterton made of the little girl's shorn hair in the peroration of his book is comparable in its eloquence with Burke's famous evocation of Marie Antoinette. It was unfortunate, therefore, that he was as careless about accuracy in his social polemics as in his literary criticism. According to Maisie Ward, Chesterton's biographer, this particular scandal turned out to be of doubtful authenticity.[41] However, there is no need to make too much of the bathos of this controversial episode, because there can really be no doubt that compulsory education and medical inspection—whatever the good intentions of those who instituted them—did, as Chesterton said, expose the poor to a degree of arbitrary tyranny astonishing in a supposedly liberal era.

The present writer came by chance upon a horrifying confirmation of this. In 1912 the appointment of Dr. Cyril Burt as the first consultant psychiatrist attached to the London education authority was noted with suspicion in the *New Witness*.[42] In 1950 the then Sir Cyril published an article in the first volume of the *British Journal of Sociology* on "The Trend of National Intelligence," in which he recalled his pioneering work on mental testing, and made it clear that the great spur to systematic testing of intelligence had been worry about the deterioration of the national stock. He explained that with the advent of compulsory education and the appointment of school medical officers, the doctors concerned had become interested in the diagnosis of "mental deficiency," and had initially regarded this as a physical problem, recognizable by smallness of skull, and possibly curable by surgery. At this point Sir Cyril added—without comment of any kind—an inconspicuous footnote to the effect that "of those operated on by Sir Victor Horsley and others (by craniectomy) twenty-five per cent died and 'those who survived showed no mental improvement.' "[43]

The reader can perhaps understand Chesterton's anger at a system of social "reform" that delivered the defenseless poor of the country into the hands of doctors who could try out their theories on these human guinea pigs, and take children from their parents on grounds of arbitrarily assessed "mental deficiency" —in order to subject them to appalling and futile operations as a result of which twenty-five per cent died, and even those who survived showed no improvement! Sir Cyril Burt gave no sign of noticing anything wrong about this, and neither did the reformers of Chesterton's own time. Caught between Tory traditionalists on the one hand, and reformers on the other, he was one of a tiny band of radical democrats who maintained that existing conditions were appallingly unjust, but that most of the supposedly philanthropic reforms were simply tyrannical.

Chesterton's chief allies in this fight were his brother Cecil and Hilaire Belloc, and the paper they started. This paper began as the *Eye-Witness* in 1911, changed its title to the *New Witness* for a long stretch of its existence (1912–23), and was eventually resurrected as *G.K.'s Weekly* (1925–36). The twin purposes of the paper were to expose corruption in public life (an aim which led to its involvement in the Marconi affair) and to campaign for "the privacy of the poor who are allowed no privacy . . . for the private property of those who have none."[44] In its early years the paper conducted vigorous campaigns against measures by the Liberal government involving regimentation of the poor. The most notable of these was Lloyd George's National Insurance Act, which involved compulsory deductions from wages, but there were plenty of others—for instance, a measure prohibiting child employment, which would (as the editor pointed out) simply reduce the income of poor families while providing no substitute, and above all the Mental Deficiency Act, which authorized any two doctors to identify any person or child as "deficient" (not insane), take him away from his family, and lock him up for life. One of the regular features of the paper was entitled "Lex v. the Poor," which drew attention to injustices, as for example the very different sentences for drunken driving imposed on gentlemanly motorists and proletarian cab drivers, or the arbitrary activities of the attendance inspectors who enforced compulsory education upon the children of the poor.

One of Chesterton's many contributions to the paper was an article published in 1917 entitled "The Evolution of Emma," in which he recalled Jane Austen's novel. Emma—an intelligent and good-hearted, but exceedingly imperious, young lady—takes it for granted that she has a right to interfere in her friend Harriet's love life, simply because she is a gentlewoman. Chesterton pointed out that the philanthropic ladies of his own day were simply carrying on that tradition of the lady of the manor, still assuming that they were entitled to run the lives of the poor by virtue of their social position alone.[45] In Chesterton's view contemporary social reform, for all its good intentions, meant regimentation for the poor, and merely underlined the fact that Britain was an oligarchical society in which freedom was reserved for the few.

He found a good opportunity to state his case in a controversy with the editor of the *Nation* in 1911. Having denounced Parliament as a thoroughly unrepresentative oligarchy, he had been asked by the editor to explain and defend his position. He replied by referring to recent measures of penal and temperance reform: "If you want examples I could give you scores. I say the people did not cry out that all children whose parents lunch on cheese and beer in an inn should be left out in the rain. I say the people did not demand that a man's sentence should be settled by his jailers instead of by his judges." The editor was rash enough to reply that the measures he had cited were "too small to prove so large a case," which gave Chesterton a perfect opening:

Why do you think of these things as small? They are really enormous. One alters the daily habits of millions of people; the other destroys the public law of thousands of years. What can be more fundamental than food, drink and children? What can be more catastrophic than putting us back in the primal anarchy, in which a man was flung into a dungeon and left there till he listened to reason?

Why do you think of these things as small? I will tell you. Unconsciously, no doubt, but simply and solely because the Front Benches did not announce them as big. They were not "first-class measures"; they were not "full-dress debates." The governing class shot them through in the quick, quiet, secondary way in which they pass things that the people positively detests. . . . going to public-houses and going to prison are both habits with which that class is, unfortunately, quite unfamiliar. It is ready, therefore, at a stroke of the pen, to bring all folly into the taverns and all injustice into the jails."[46]

2. Freedom and the Pub

The right of the poor to drink or not to drink, as they themselves decided, was one of the causes with which Chesterton was most conspicuously associated, particularly after the publication of *The Flying Inn* in 1914. This novel is a fantasy about an England upon which prohibition has been imposed by a fanatical aristocrat, Lord Ivywood, under the influence of a Moslem charlatan. He is defied by an English innkeeper and an Irish sailor, who wander the length and breadth of England with their mobile inn sign and cask of rum, and at last raise the people against Ivywood and his garrison of Turkish troops. The novel has little to recommend it except a collection of rousing drinking songs, which include the well-known poem about how "the rolling English drunkard made the rolling English road," and:

Old Noah he had an ostrich farm and fowls on the largest
    scale,
He ate his egg with a ladle in an egg-cup big as a pail,
And the soup he took was Elephant Soup and the fish he took
    was Whale,
But they all were small to the cellar he took when he set out
    to sail,
And Noah he often said to his wife when he sat down to dine,
"I don't care where the water goes if it doesn't get into
    the wine."[47]

As a result of such poems, Chesterton acquired a reputation as a roaring drunkard. However, while he was certainly fond of his glass of wine, the defense of the right to drink meant more to him than the championship of one particular pleasure. It represented on the one hand the liberty of the poor, and on the other what seemed to him a sane and Christian attitude to life, which was under attack from the fads of his time.

His first argument against temperance was simply that it was a class measure, imposed by the rich upon the poor. Since the foundation of the United Kingdom Alliance in 1853, temperance reformers had become an increasingly vocal section of the Liberal Party, and their campaign was gaining momentum in Britain as in America. These reformers were themselves usually total abstainers, and were to that extent prepared to suffer the same rigors that they imposed upon others. However, as Chesterton continually pointed out, the effects of prohibition were different for different classes. Closing down public houses, or reducing their opening hours, affected only the poor, whereas the rich could—and did—get drunk at home, if necessary by having alcohol prescribed as "medicine."

It was natural enough that the reformers should be horrified by the prevalence of drunkenness and squalor in the slums, especially by the spectacle of money being wasted on drink when families were so poor: but their remedy was to make it impossible for the poor to exercise any freedom of choice at all—to demand from them an iron rigidity in managing what tiny resources they had, never allowing any spontaneous impulse. A typical such reformer was Beveridge, who was prominent in laying the foundations of the welfare state. When critics of the National Insurance Act argued that the unskilled could not afford the compulsory contributions, he replied that such people already spent the equivalent amount of money "on luxuries with which they could well dispense."[48] It was in response to this kind of self-righteous puritanism on other people's behalf that Chesterton defended drink as the sole luxury of the poor.

But besides this right of every man to some area of choice, however small, Chesterton also defended the pub as an institution, the working man's club. The desire for talk, comradeship, and democratic society he regarded as a basic masculine characteristic. Some of the more sensitive temperance reformers, such as Joseph Rowntree, did recognize that if the pubs were to be closed the working men would lose their social life. However, their suggestion for a substitute was, inevitably, a "People's Palace" that would provide instructive lectures over the cocoa. In other words, yet more paternalism was to replace the rough democracy of the public house.[49]

Chesterton opposed temperance reform, then, in the name of the few liberties of the poor. Yet it is only fair to point out that, while the ranks of the teetotalers certainly contained many industrialists who had an interest in a sober and disciplined work force, they also included large numbers of labor leaders and genuine working men, who had quite as much of the Nonconformist conscience as their social superiors. Chesterton's implied contrast between the upper class authoritarian, and the working man with his spontaneous comradeship in the pub, is a considerable oversimplification. However, there was another side to his championship of drinking, connected with both his populism and his Christianity. It seemed to him that the upper classes of his time must be opposed, not only because they were oligarchic and meddling, but also because their "progressive" principles and ideas had left the broad track of sanity, common sense, and Christianity.

To Chesterton, Christianity represented above all two essential values: first, the sacredness of every man, woman, and child, regardless of their class, education, or "eugenic fitness"; second, the goodness of human nature and the world in spite of their faults, mysteries, and contradictions. When looking at *Orthodoxy,* we saw that Chesterton had come to the conclusion that Christianity was true because it was comprehensive and commonsensical: because its mysteries and apparent incoherencies only reflected ordinary human experience. One of the constant themes of his writings was that the defense of Christian orthodoxy against heresies of one sort or another had always been the defense of this apparently muddled, but actually sane, common ground, against the grand simplifying ideas of the heresiarchs. Heresies were seductive because they were always clear, simple, and rational: but they were always too simple to be true, for in each case they took one good idea too far, and ignored the rest of reality.

The example Chesterton quoted most frequently was Islam, which he regarded as a Christian heresy. It was much simpler than Christianity, much easier to state and understand, much more intellectually coherent. But in its belief in fate, its ascetic prohibition of alcohol, and its ban on pictures and statues, it denied the things orthodox Christianity had always asserted—that worldly and material things are, in a flawed and complex way, *good* things, and that the glory of humanity lies in being free to set its own limits to their use. This desire for simplicity at the expense of fidelity to common experience seemed to Chesterton to have posed a recurrent threat to Christian society, manifested for instance in the medieval Albigensian heresy and in Calvinistic Puritanism.

He found signs of this puritanical desire for rationalistic simplicity not only in the Nonconformist temperance movement but in many of the post-Christian fads of his time, such as the vegetarianism popular in advanced circles and practiced most notably by Bernard Shaw. In a witty and perceptive study of Shaw published in 1909, he emphasized both Shaw's rationalistic Puritanism and his disdainful separation from common people and common things. He remarked that it was a great mistake to suppose that Shaw's opinions were paradoxical:

... if by paradox we mean truth inherent in a contradiction ... it is a very curious fact that Bernard Shaw is almost entirely without paradox.... All his splendid vistas and startling suggestions arise from carrying some one clear principle further than it has yet been carried. His madness is all consistency, not inconsistency.[50]

Shaw's socialism, his vegetarianism, his antipatriotism, his notion of nonauthoritarian education—all seemed to Chesterton cases of a single simple idea being carried to its logical conclusion, undeterred by common sense.

From the crazy single-mindedness of progressive opinion, Chesterton appealed to the solid common sense of the working man. The confrontation he had in mind was epitomized by an anecdote that he included in his *Autobiography*. It concerned a lady vegetarian and the wife of Will Crooks, "the only Labour leader I ever knew who reminded me for a single moment of the English labouring classes." The vegetarian, "an ethereal little lady with pale blue eyes and pale green garments," heard a politician, Noel Buxton, remarking that in the bustle of electioneering he had barely had time to snatch a cutlet for lunch.

... the prophetess in the green garments was goaded, by the god within her, to speak. When Buxton had left the room she did so.

"Do you think that was really necessary?" she said with a painful fixity, like one in a trance. "Man is no better for a cutlet. Man does not really need cutlets."

At this point she received hearty, one might almost say heavy support, from what was probably an unexpected quarter.

"No, my dear," said Mrs. Crooks in resounding tones, "a man doesn't want a cutlet. What's the good of a cutlet? What a man wants is a good chump chop or a bit of the under-cut; and I'd see he got it."

The other lady sighed; it was not quite what she had meant; and she was obviously a little alarmed to advance again against her large and solid opponent and be felled to the earth with a mutton-bone. But that little comedy of cross-purposes has always remained in my memory, as a perfect parable of the two kinds of simple life, the false and the true.[51]

Vegetarianism and other such fads of advanced opinion might seem merely amusing, except when the fanatics of progress attempted to impose their ideals upon the poor. But the worship of science that was so characteristic of educated circles took forms that Chesterton recognized as positive evils, to be fought with all his strength. The most considerable of these was eugenics.

3. Eugenics

The notion of setting out to breed a superior race of men and to eliminate the "unfit" now smells so strongly of Nazism that any such suggestion is guaranteed to cause an outcry. It is all the more necessary, therefore, to recognize that we owe a bitterly ironic debt to Hitler for making eugenics so disreputable: before World War II it was an eminently respectable policy, put forward enthusiastically in all the "advanced" nations by scientific experts who considered themselves friends to humanity.

In the late nineteenth century, in the wake of Darwin and Mendel, there was intense interest in evolution and genetics. In view of the prestige of science, and the decline of Christianity among the educated, it was natural that the idea of applying science to the improvement of human society should be popular. The science of eugenics was developed initially by Francis Galton (1822–1911) and his followers. Its basic principle was that, as in the case of animals, so also in the case of human beings, inherited qualities are all-important. Good care and feeding can of course enable any particular cow or pig to develop to the limit of its potential, but farmers are well aware that the way to get good cattle is to improve the strain by selective breeding. In the wild, the process of natural selection improves breeds to suit their environment, because the weaker die off or fail to reproduce themselves; but the deliberate breeding practiced by the farmer is less haphazard and more humane.

According to the eugenists, precisely the same considerations must be applied to human beings. Men had evolved from apes as a result of a long and brutal process of natural selection. Under conditions of civilization, however, natural selection no longer applied. It was now possible deliberately to encourage the breeding of the highest human type, and furthermore it was becoming more and more necessary to do so, because humanitarian social policies prevented the unfit from being weeded out, and indeed encouraged them to propagate themselves and to swamp the race with inferior genes. It comes as no surprise to find that the "unfit" was usually taken to mean the lower classes, especially paupers, and the "fit" to mean the wealthy and educated.

A quasi-religious concern for the future of the race was often sharpened by the fear—extremely widespread among the British upper classes in the first forty years of this century—that the British stock was declining. The very poor physical condition of many army recruits during the Boer War set off this anxiety, which was increased by the discovery about the same time that the highest classes—usually presumed to be the "fittest"—had the lowest birth rate, while births were most frequent among those taken to be the eugenic dregs of the nation.[52] Toward the end of his long life, Galton himself wrote that the first object of eugenics was "to check the birth-rate of the unfit. . . . The *second* object is the improvement of the race by furthering the productivity of the fit by early marriages and healthful rearing of their children."[53]

Karl Pearson, Galton's disciple, and Professor of Eugenics at London University, declared in 1912: "The death-rate is selective, and if we check Nature's effective but roughshod methods of race betterment, we must take her task into our own hands and see to it that the mentally and physically inferior have not a dominant fertility."[54] Pearson suggested a number of very drastic remedies, which amounted to leaving paupers, tramps, and the insane to starve; for "if we leave the fertile, but unfit, one sixth to reproduce half the next generation, our nation will soon cease to be a world power."

Eugenic ideas were at the height of their popularity when Huxley wrote *Brave New World* in 1932. One book which had a very respectful reception was *The Survival of the Unfittest* by Charles Wicksteed Armstrong,[55] which attacked unemployment relief on eugenic grounds. Armstrong declared that "the nation which first begins to *breed for efficiency*—denying the right of the scum to beget millions of their kind . . . is the nation destined to rule the earth."[56] Consequently the poor, and especially those who were mentally defective, must be prevented from breeding. He further observed that "to diminish the dangerous fertility of the unfit there are three methods: the lethal chamber, segregation and sterilization."[57] He recommended an official eugenic classification of the population, after which A-1s would be given tax privileges to enable them to have more children, whereas C-3s would be sterilized or segregated.

Armstrong and many other eugenists saw welfare legislation and humanitarian philanthropy as the enemies of a sound racial stock. Many of the social reformers, however, saw no such incompatibility, and eugenic considerations were interwoven with much of the legislation that lies at the foundations of the welfare state.[58] For instance, compulsory medical inspection in schools, and the provision of homes for physical and mental defectives, were prompted not only by concern for the care of such children, but also by anxiety to shut them up so that they could not reproduce. One piece of mythology that loomed particularly large in the progressive mind was the belief that people of low intellectual powers actually have a higher natural physical fertility than other people. This was one of the chief arguments for the Mental Deficiency Act, authorizing lifelong incarceration on the word of two doctors, against which the *New Witness* waged a lonely battle.[59]

To its credit, the Roman Catholic Church denounced eugenics from the start. But outside what was generally regarded as a blindly reactionary body, the weight of progressive opinion found few opponents, and Chesterton—who took up his position long before becoming a Roman Catholic—was one of the most notable. In *Eugenics and Other Evils,* published in 1922, he confronted head on a movement that seemed to him to sum up the wickedness and injustice of his time.

In the first part of the book, Chesterton attacked the theory of eugenics with great liveliness and lucidity. In particular, he was careful to make clear what its high-sounding theories were bound to mean in practice: "Eugenics, as discussed, evidently means the control of some men over the marriage and unmarriage of others; and probably means the control of the few over the marriage and unmarriage of the many."[60] Whatever the protests of idealistic or muddled eugenists, this could not be other than a staggering attack on human rights, obviously incompatible with any pretense of democracy. It must entail putting power over domestic life into the hands of a few, while the sheer vagueness of notions about eugenic "fitness" or otherwise would make the exercise of this power utterly arbitrary. Chesterton cited here the case of the Mental Deficiency Act providing for the incarceration of the feeble-minded—which was not only tyrannical in itself, but obviously wide open to abuse: "My point is that if I want to dispossess a nephew, oust a rival, silence a blackmailer, or get rid of an importunate widow, there is nothing in logic to prevent my calling them feeble-minded too. And the vaguer the charge is the less they will be able to disprove it."[61] Eugenists tended to assume that the officials administering such laws would be perfect and incorruptible—an illusion to which Chesterton was not subject.

The eugenic movement seemed to Chesterton to be part of the encroaching new tyranny of science. He remarked that zealous Liberal Nonconformists were wasting their efforts fighting against the waning power of the Established Church of England:

The thing that really is trying to tyrannise through government is Science. The thing that really does use the secular arm is Science. And the creed that really is levying tithes and capturing schools, the creed that really is enforced by fine and imprisonment, the creed that really is proclaimed not in sermons but in statutes, and spread not by pilgrims but by policemen—that creed is the great but disputed system of thought which began in Evolution and has ended in Eugenics.[62]

Furthermore, the scientific experts now gaining power were in one respect even worse than the Inquisition, for they did not even pretend to know the truth. They craved power in order to experiment on the population, as in the proposals that were already being made—and that were later carried out by the Nazis—for the vivisection of criminals.

However, the principal danger of eugenics seemed to Chesterton to lie less in the misguided doctors who propagated it than in the class interests it served. In Part II of his book, entitled "The Real Aim," he maintained that "at root the Eugenist is the Employer."[63] As he pointed out, no one was suggesting that the marriages of the rich should be controlled, even though aristocrats, with their long recorded pedigrees, would surely afford the greatest scope for scientific investigation. But this field "remains unexplored not merely through snobbery and cowardice, but because the Eugenist (at least the influential Eugenist) half-consciously knows it is no part of his job; what he is really wanted for is to get the grip of the governing classes on to the unmanageable output of poor people."[64]

Eugenics, in fact, was being taken up enthusiastically because it offered a solution to the problem that capitalists had created for themselves: what to do with the masses of wretched, half-starved, stunted "unemployables" in the slums of the great cities. Its explanation was to be found in the history of the English poor, of which Chesterton gave his own version in an eloquent chapter entitled "True History of a Tramp." He pointed out that the poor had always been exploited—as slave, serf, and proletarian; but at least in earlier times the slave was fed by his master, the serf had a field to till. The peculiar cruelty of modern conditions was that the poor man was just as unequal and exploited, but he had lost even the vestige of security enjoyed by his ancestors. If he was one of the thousands of tramps who were continually harassed by the police for sleeping beside the river Thames in London, he was utterly destitute. He had no land, no home, no work, no money, no right even to

sleep on the bare earth by night, without being collared by a policeman. . . . A little while ago two tramps were summoned before a magistrate, charged with sleeping in the open air when they had nowhere else to sleep. But this is not the full fun of the incident. The real fun is that each of them eagerly produced about twopence, to prove that they could have got a bed, but deliberately didn't. To which the policeman replied that twopence would not have got them a bed: that they could not possibly have got a bed: and therefore (argued that thoughtful officer) they ought to be punished for not getting one. The intelligent magistrate was much struck with the argument: and proceeded to imprison these two men for not doing a thing they could not do.[65]

Chesterton argued that, having produced a vast mass of destitute and wretched people, the employers were now alarmed at what they had done, and concerned especially that so many children should be growing up stunted and unemployable. However, rather than put the capitalist machine into reverse, or give the poor enough money to live on decently, the response of the governing class was to use police powers to control their breeding. What seemed particularly shocking to Chesterton was that such gross infractions of human rights should be contemplated or unopposed by *Liberals*. The Liberals of his generation appeared to have lost all conception of liberty, at any rate where the poor were concerned.

In Chesterton's view, the new liberalism combined all the evils of capitalism and socialism simultaneously.

In short, people decided that it was impossible to achieve any of the good of Socialism, but they comforted themselves by achieving all the bad. All that official discipline, about which the Socialists themselves were in doubt or at least on the defensive, was taken over bodily by the Capitalists. They have now added all the bureaucratic tyrannies of a Socialist state to the old plutocratic tyrannies of a Capitalist state. For the vital point is that it did not in the smallest degree diminish the inequalities of a Capitalist State. It simply destroyed such individual liberties as remained among its victims. It did not enable any man to build a better house; it only limited the houses he might live in—or how he might manage to live there; forbidding him to keep pigs or poultry or to sell beer or cider. It did not even add anything to a man's wages; it only took away something from a man's wages, and locked it up, whether he liked it or not, in a sort of money-box which

71

was regarded as a medicine-chest. It does not send food into the house to feed the children; it only sends an inspector into the house to punish the parents for having no food to feed them. It does not see that they have got a fire; it only punishes them for not having a fire-guard. It does not even occur to it to provide the fire-guard.[66]

This spirit of scientific regimentation in the interests of a ruling class seemed to Chesterton to be typified by Germany, and he remarked in the Preface to *Eugenics* that he had hoped that the war would put an end to such tendencies in England. However, he found that even after the defeat of Germany, the same influences still needed to be combated. Later, in the 1930s, he was saddened but not surprised by the rise of Nazism, which seemed to him to represent precisely the modern barbarism against which he had been warning for so long.

4. The Servile State in Retrospect

Let us conclude this chapter by looking at modern Britain, and considering the present state of the causes for which Chesterton fought. The first point to be made is that the triumph of the social legislation he opposed has not in fact resulted, as he and Belloc expected, in a "servile state." For it is important to realize that they did not mean by this phrase simply a country with a lot of bureaucratic regulation. They meant something much more precise and objectionable: namely, a system under which the proletariat were subject to regulation from which their masters were exempt, and under which they were compelled to work, with no right to organize or strike, as the price of a minimum of social security. In other words, Belloc and Chesterton expected the drift toward bureaucratic regulation to be accompanied by an increase in formalized inequality, separating the workers from the capitalists and creating two classes with quite different legal status and rights. Like the Marxist predictions of increasing polarization between classes, this expectation has not been borne out. While it would be foolish to suggest that workers in any industrial country enjoy equality with millionaires, there can be no doubt that they resemble a servile class very much less now than in Chesterton's time. Ordinary people are not only better off in material terms; perhaps even more significantly, they have higher status, they are accorded more dignity, and they have greater political influence than in Chesterton's day. And these achievements must be attributed largely to the labor movement, that is to say, not only to the vastly increased influence of trade unionists, with whom Chesterton strongly sympathized, but also to the Socialist politicians whom he despised.

Were he alive today, Chesterton could certainly point to a vast growth in official interference with people's lives, much of it of an indefensible kind.* However, the actual administration of the ever-growing social services is certainly much *less* tyrannical in its effect upon ordinary people than in his time, mainly because bureaucratic authority is no longer so strongly reinforced by the social gulf that separated ladies and gentlemen from "persons." Similarly, while plutocrats are a hardy race and show no sign of becoming extinct, the government of a country such as Britain is much less a matter of inbred cliques of the rich than in Chesterton's day. Modern British democracy could hardly be described as rule by the common man, but it has certainly become more rather than less democratic.

As we have seen, Chesterton made much of the desire of the ordinary man for a house of his own, and the determination of the reformers as well as the Conservatives to deny him this. His strictures would be very appropriate to the postwar rehousing of thousands of British city dwellers in tower blocks. These blocks were never popular with anyone except the architects and town planners—who did not choose to live in them themselves—and recently even the experts have concluded that they were a colos-

* The recent appointment, by an enlightened local authority in England, of an expert to remedy "educational deprivation" by going into houses in the area to teach mothers to talk to their babies, cries out for his mockery.

sal mistake. In spite of the persistence of this kind of misguided paternalism, however, it is true to say that vastly more British families now have their own houses than would have seemed possible in 1910. True, these houses are hardly the citadels of independence that Chesterton dreamed of, being either rented from the local authority, or "owner-occupied" on the strength of a lifelong mortgage. Still, they do provide more scope for the joys of domesticity than the slums of Chesterton's day.

Since that time, however, the whole meaning of domesticity has been transformed by the emancipation of women. No other aspect of Chesterton's outlook seems so utterly outdated as his views on women and their proper place: it is impossible to see his pronouncements on the different characteristics of the two sexes as anything but thoroughly misleading generalizations. The camaraderie he attributed to men, and the reticence he ascribed to women, are certainly genuine aspects of human nature, of which it is illuminating to have such vivid descriptions: but it is evidently false to suggest that all men possess the one, or all women the other.[67]

It is a pity that Chesterton tied his defense of home, family, and domestic life so closely to his claims about male and female characteristics, since it is precisely this kind of assertion that has made so many radicals assume that the liberation of women is impossible without the destruction of the family. In another area Chesterton did a service by pointing out that opposition to large-scale capitalism does not entail condemnation of small private property; a parallel position can be plausibly argued where domesticity is concerned. For the persistence of the family does not necessarily imply the subjection of women, and conversely, women's liberation need not mean communal living. As Chesterton pointed out, making a home and caring for children can mean a much more interesting and less restrictive life than most modern jobs. And now that role-changing between husbands and wives is becoming socially acceptable, both men and women are discovering that, when domesticity is not an inescapable doom, it becomes not a restriction but an opportunity. However, this new form of flexible domesticity has been made possible only through the spread of contraception, to which Chesterton was as strongly opposed as he was to eugenics, and for much the same reasons.

The modern fate of eugenics in Britain is interesting.[68] As a result of the traumatic experience of Nazism, modern eugenists couch their proposals in more circumspect and defensive terms than in Chesterton's day. However, their dreams of solving the problems of the human race by genetic engineering do not seem to have changed much. They are still prone to the illusion that if men and women were bred to be fitter and more intelligent, they would also, by some quite unexplained process, become less competitive, cruel, and destructive. To that extent, Chesterton's strictures on eugenic utopias are still entirely relevant. However, since his time the vast increases in medical knowledge have created new moral problems, to which his robust traditionalism provides no more guidance than does science itself. The medical ability to preserve lives that were formerly doomed has resulted not only in the increasing threat of overpopulation, but also in new dilemmas, such as whether to use elaborate methods to keep hopelessly ill people alive. Faced with such decisions, neither expert opinion nor common sense is much help.

Chesterton's faith in the common sense of ordinary people is likely to seem most startling to readers now. We have become accustomed to accept as a platitude that liberals are those few educated people who hold "advanced" opinions, whereas ordinary people, being less educated, are reactionary. Consequently it is frequently argued that the preservation of liberal and "democratic" values depends upon representative systems which *prevent* the mass of the people from having much influence on policy.[69] Similarly, we tend to see nothing odd in governments carrying through "liberal" legislation in the teeth of popular opposition, whether it is the abolition of capital punishment in Britain or the integration of school children by bussing in America. Chesterton, however, did not accept this viewpoint, and regarded the rule of self-styled progressives as a new and particularly vexatious form of tyranny over the poor.

His own ideal was and remained a democratic republic of a more or less Rousseauian kind: literal self-government by ordinary men, each of them secure and independent in possession of his own land or workshop, ruling themselves through equal laws. He revered the self-governing cities of the Middle Ages, and caught from Hilaire Belloc a romantic veneration for the French Revolution and the democratic tradition it had left behind. It represented for him one of the few occasions when the ordinary people of a country had rebelled against the intricate injustices and mystifications of aristocrats in order to assert common interests and common sense:

We, the modern English, cannot easily understand the French Revolution, because we cannot easily understand the idea of bloody battle for pure common sense; we cannot understand common sense in arms and conquering. In modern England common sense appears to mean putting up with existing conditions. For us a practical politician really means a man who can be thoroughly trusted to do nothing at all; that is where his practicality comes in. The French feeling—the feeling at the back of the Revolution—was that the more sensible a man was, the more you must look out for slaughter.[70]

In appealing to "the people" against an oligarchy, Chesterton shared with other democrats a disposition to regard the people as the custodians of "common sense," "human nature," and similarly vague though admirable qualities. In his case as in all others, this creates two connected problems. The most obvious is the problem of identifying "the people." Who are they, and how does one recognize them? But the other problem is equally recalcitrant: if the qualities that the people have constitute common sense and human feelings, how is it that these are not universal and triumphant? How does one account for the defeat of human nature and common sense in so many human societies? Generally speaking, Chesterton's answer to such questions would be that he spoke for ordinary Christian people against an intellectual elite who had been led astray by false doctrines and oligarchic interests; but the problem of identifying "the people" remains, particularly since Chesterton was a notably independent man who would never have dreamed of running with the mob. As it happened, many of Chesterton's opinions were widely shared in England. However, his antiimperialism certainly was not, and the Boer War—in opposition to which he first found his political stance—was wildly popular until it began to go badly. Clearly, Chesterton's appeal to the people did not imply simple endorsement of anything that the majority happened to think.

When he talked about "the people," the concrete image upon which he most frequently drew was that of the ordinary gregarious working man in his pub, and this immediately highlights the problem of identification. For one of the conspicuous features of the English labor movement has been that the men who represented the working class—in the sense of becoming trade union leaders or Labour members of Parliament—tended not to conform to that comfortable image, being very often Nonconformist, teetotal, self-educated, and similar in outlook to the Liberal social reformers. Chesterton was sometimes inclined to dismiss most Labour MPs as mere social climbers, but he showed greater sensitivity on the issue in a novel published at the time of the General Strike, *The Return of Don Quixote*. One of its main characters is a militant syndicalist trade union leader called Braintree, a self-educated and very intelligent man who can hold his own and preach his case eloquently in an aristocratic drawing room. However, when he is taken on a pub crawl—by an aristocrat of wide sympathies and gregarious habits—he finds himself miserably out of place: he can represent the interests of the ordinary man at work, but he cannot enter into or sympathize with the working man's pleasures. Nevertheless, it is clear from the novel that Chesterton is far from intending to expose him as a fraud, or to suggest that he has no right to his red revolutionary tie. On the contrary, Braintree is one of the more sympathetic characters in this very complex novel.

Chesterton himself realized, therefore, that his picture of the masculine camaraderie of the public house was not all-inclusive, and that the kind of sensitive but frigid individualism which he attributed so sweepingly to women was not simply a sexual characteristic. Democratic theories can often be criticized for assuming that everyone is to all intents and purposes alike. They do not allow for people being different, especially for those sensitive intellectuals who are aware of being very different indeed. John Stuart Mill would certainly have shuddered at Chesterton's vision of democratic self-government by the regulars of all the pubs in England. However, the short answer to this objection is that—in England, at any rate—there has never been any need to take elaborate precautions against rule by the man in the pub, because there has never been the slightest danger of anything so democratic. The actual danger in England has always been rule by an oligarchy who thought of themselves as not only richer and more powerful, but also more intelligent and advanced, than the rest of the population. The point of Chesterton's appeal to the people, and his insistence on their rights, was that they were in danger of being ignored altogether.

The peculiar difficulty of any populist position is that it does not merely appeal to the people as the source of authority and deny the claims of oligarchy: it also assumes that the people stand for whatever the writer regards as fundamental and uncorrupted human nature. Chesterton articulated sentiments that he claimed were the common feelings of common men—democracy, domesticity, the desire for property—and set these against the values of intellectuals and businessmen. As we shall see in the next chapter, however, the acid test of Chesterton's claim to interpret the popular mood was Distributism. For the Distributist League, which intended to restore the land to the people, never became at all a popular movement. Must we conclude, then, that Chesterton's defense of the common man was spurious? His disciples might perhaps argue that he could not have enjoyed such vast popularity as a writer and broadcaster if he had not expressed the feelings of most people. But the fallacy of such an argument can easily be shown by applying it simultaneously to Shaw, whose views were quite different. The fact is, anyone who can write as entertainingly as Shaw or Chesterton will have an audience, whatever views he maintains.

Nevertheless, it is true that Chesterton's writings did answer a need, and articulate important and neglected human feelings. His defense of equality and human dignity, of home and family, of property and privacy, was important in his own time, and continues to be so now, because it gave articulate form and intellectual respectability to values that correspond to widespread human sentiments, but that were in danger of being submerged beneath the tide of educated opinion. The virtue of Chesterton's writing is not that it represents the sole truth about the moral and social requirements of human nature, but that it redresses the balance by attacking the orthodoxies of his time in the name of values that were real but neglected. Chesterton did a service to social and political discussions by raising to the status of clear and articulate principles, values that were so unfashionable that they lingered only as popular prejudices, of which the people themselves were half ashamed. As he wrote of the working class in *Eugenics:*

... they are under the enormous disadvantage of being right without knowing it. They hold their sound principles as if they were sullen prejudices. .... Often a poor woman will tell a magistrate that she sticks to her husband, with the defiant and desperate air of a wanton resolved to run away from her husband. Often she will cry as hopelessly, and as it were helplessly, when deprived of her child as if she were a child deprived of her doll.[71]

4

Peasant and Patriot

. . . Mightier to me the house my fathers made
Than your audacious heads, O Halls of Rome!
More than immortal marbles undecayed
The thin sad slates that cover up my home.[1]

Chesterton's political thought is profoundly emotional. This is not
to say that it is irrational, nor that he indulged in shallow
demagoguery. On the contrary, his rhetoric is always argumenta-
tive, and his eloquence generally makes more effective the defense of a perfectly rational position. His political thought is
emotional in that it is built upon a sympathy with the deeply
rooted human emotions that cluster round the home and the
homeland: the love of an ordinary man not only for his family
but for his home; the longing for a little domain of one's own,
whether it be a peasant's land or a suburban clerk's garden, or
even a slum dweller's back yard; the loyalty of men to their own
country and their willingness to fight for it.

Most of the political views of Chesterton's time seemed to him
either to ignore these basic loves and loyalties, or to seek deliberately to crush them. This was obvious in the case of socialism. The communistic and cosmopolitian idealism of the Socialists, while seeking to unite all mankind, would not allow any
particular man anything to be loyal to, whether his own house or
his own country. But it seemed to Chesterton that precisely the
same was true of Tory imperialism, whose praise of private

property meant, in practice, praise of gigantic monopolistic corporations, and whose patriotism seemed to mean dying for enormous and amorphous entities like the British Empire or the Anglo-Saxon race. Chesterton insisted that the things men can be profoundly loyal to are *small* things. The natural human desire is not for a barracks but for a house of one's own, in support of which he quoted the Labour MP, Will Crooks: "The most sacred thing is to be able to shut your own door."[2] A man wants not a trackless wilderness but a plot of land, preferably with a good thick hedge round it; not an empire on which the sun never sets, but a small, familiar land with visible frontiers.

This sense of the value of small, clearly limited things is a constant motif in his writings, with aesthetic as well as political implications. For instance, he drew an effective contrast between the medieval art of illumination—"little pictures where the blue sky is hardly larger than a single sapphire"—and the gigantic and all-too-vivid modern posters advertising Reckitt's Blue and Colman's Mustard.[3] In his *Autobiography,* remembering the magic of his father's homemade toy theater and the miniature dramas enacted on its miniscule stage, he remarked: "All my life I have loved frames and limits; and I will maintain that the largest wilderness looks larger seen through a window."[4] And this insight—that the things which are most precious to men are small rather than large, and definitely fenced about rather than amorphous—this fundamental diagnosis of human emotions remained with him all his life, and has a great deal to do with his social and political standpoint. In this chapter we shall be concerned with two major strands within this line of thought: first, his scheme of property for all, clumsily labeled Distributism; second, his antiimperialist patriotism.

1. Property for All

It is calmly assumed that the only two possible types of society are a Collectivist type of society and the type of society that exists at this moment and is rather like an animated muck-heap. It is quite un-necessary to say that I should prefer Socialism to the present state of things. I should prefer anarchism to the present state of things. But it is simply not the fact that Collectivism is the only other scheme for a more equal order.[5]

The first thing to grasp about Distributism, the social policy advocated by Belloc, Cecil Chesterton, and Chesterton himself, is that it was an exceedingly radical policy. When, in the period of industrial strife and social ferment just before World War I, Belloc and Chesterton wrote for the *Daily Herald,* there was nothing specially incongruous in their presence among the variegated radicals, syndicalists, guild socialists, and others who found in the *Herald* a platform from which to attack equally the Liberal government and the halting compromises of the parliamentary Labour Party. They were in no sense defenders of the status quo, and their writings and journalism are as full of the rhetoric of revolution as those of any Marxist. However, they were almost as strongly opposed to socialism as to capital-ism, taking the line that what was wrong with the latter was not that there was too much respect for property, but too little. What characteristically happened in capitalist countries was that all small property and small businesses were swallowed up by more and more gigantic monopolies, so that the vast majority of the population became dependent upon organizations socialist in their scale though not in their social conscience.

Chesterton effectively ridiculed the supposed virtues of rugged individualism fostered by capitalism:

> The reader refolds the *Daily Mail* and rises from his intensely in-dividualistic breakfast-table, where he has just dispatched his bold and adventurous breakfast; the bacon cut in rashers from the wild boar which but lately turned to bay in his back garden; the eggs perilously snatched from swaying nest and flapping bird at the top of those toppling trees which gave the house its appropriate name of Pine Crest. He puts on his own curious and creative hat, built on some bold plan entirely made up out of his own curious and creative

head. He walks outside his unique and unparalleled house, also built with his own well-won wealth according to his own well-conceived architectural design, and seeming by its very outline against the sky to express his own passionate personality. He strides down the street, making his own way over hill and dale towards the place of his own chosen and favourite labour, the workshop of his imaginative craft. He lingers on the way, now to pluck a flower, now to compose a poem, for his time is his own; he is an individual and a free man and not as these Communists. . . . Such is the life of the clerk in a world of private enterprise and practical individualism.[6]

The answer to the evils of monopoly, he maintained, was not more monopoly and centralization, but less:

> I am one of those who believe that the cure for centralisation is de-centralisation. It has been described as a paradox. There is apparently something elvish and fantastic about saying that when capital has come to be too much in the hands of the few, the right thing is to re-store it into the hands of the many. The Socialist would put it in the hands of even fewer; but those people would be politicians, who (as we know) always administer it in the interests of the many.[7]

What the Distributists wished to do, therefore, was on the one hand to strengthen and support such small farmers, shop-keepers, and independent craftsmen as remained, and on the other hand to create a new class of small proprietors by breaking up big estates and big enterprises. Inevitably, they were accused of flying in the face of progress, science, and efficiency, and Chesterton devoted a good deal of his main book on the subject, *The Outline of Sanity,* to answering this charge. As the next chapter will show in more detail, he thought it a characteristically modern and quite unjustified superstition to believe that mankind is doomed to "progress," and cannot retrace its steps after taking a wrong turning. Capitalism seemed to him obviously a mistake, since its unprecented wealth had in fact generated poverty for the vast majority of the population.

He poured scorn on the supposedly superior efficiency of large department stores over small shops, large estates over small peasant farms. Ireland represented for him a practical demonstration of Distributism, since successive British governments, in the course of their uncertain mixture of coercion and conciliation toward the Irish, had gradually given Irish tenant farmers greater security of tenure, and then, after Wyndham's Land Purchase Act of 1903, bought out the landlords in order to establish the tenants as independent proprietors. When Chesterton visited Ireland during World War I, he was impressed by the results. He described a particularly vivid contrast between the "progressive" and "reactionary" social systems manifesting themselves on opposite sides of one country road:

I was moving in a hired motor down a road in the North-West, towards the middle of that rainy autumn. . . . But what struck my mind and stuck in it was this; that all down one side of the road, as far as we went, the harvest was gathered in neatly and safely; and all down the other side of the road it was rotting in the rain. Now the side where it was safe was a string of small plots worked by peasant proprietors, as petty by our standards as a row of the cheapest villas. The land on which all the harvest was wasted was the land of a large modern estate. I asked why the landlord was later with his harvesting than the peasants; and I was told rather vaguely that there had been strikes and similar labour troubles. I did not go into the rights of the matter; but the point here is that, whatever they were, the moral is the same. You may curse the cruel Capitalist landlord or you may rave at the ruffianly Bolshevist strikers; but you must admit that between them they have produced a stoppage, which the peasant proprietorship a few yards off did not produce. . . .

For it must be sharply realised that the peasant proprietors succeeded here, not only because they were really proprietors, but because they were only peasants. It was because they were on a small scale that they were a great success. It was because they were too poor to have servants that they grew rich in spite of strikers. It was, so far as it went, the flattest possible contradiction to all that is said in England, both by Collectivists and Capitalists, about the efficiency of the great organisation. For in so far as it had failed, it had actually failed, not only through being great, but through being organised. On

84

the left side of the road the big machine had stopped working, *because* it was a big machine. The small men were still working, because they were not machines.[8]

Chesterton was not prepared to concede, then, that large-scale organization was efficient, and small-scale tradesmen or peasants inefficient. Neither was he prepared to accept the common assumption that the life of such small proprietors is narrow, and that large-scale industrialism is an enlarging and liberating force. "I know it is said that a man must find it monotonous to do the twenty things that are done on a farm, whereas, of course, he always finds it uproariously funny and festive to do one thing hour after hour and day after day in a factory."[9] As for the cultural effects of small proprietorship, he pointed to peasant dances, costumes, and crafts, and to the mystery plays and ceremonies of the medieval guilds, all of which compared well with the mass culture of modern society.

Chesterton's initial claim, then, was that capitalism and socialism were not the only alternatives, and that small proprietorship could not simply be dismissed as "reactionary." Such proprietorship seemed to him not only a possible escape route from modern crises but a positively desirable ideal, because only in a society of small proprietors could all men share an equal human dignity, and because only small proprietorship could satisfy natural human feelings.

His continual criticism of the society in which he lived resolves itself into one fundamental point: the incompatability of riches and poverty with the fundamental equality of men. His most passionately held moral and political belief was that all men, rich or poor, clever or stupid, were equally the images of God, entitled to equal liberties, equal consideration, and equal dignity; but it was evidently impossible that they should enjoy such equal rights in a society with extremes of riches and poverty. The destitute tramp was treated as a criminal whatever he did, whereas the plutocrat was never treated as a criminal no matter what *he* did. A modicum of property for all seemed to him the only possible basis for the recognition of equal human rights; as he constantly pointed out, in this respect the situation of many people had actually got worse in the ages of progress and enlightenment. Both the modern tramp and the medieval serf were subject to arbitrary power, but at least the serf had access to the means of production. In *The Outline of Sanity* he cited the story of Jack and the Beanstalk: "That story begins with the strange and startling words, 'There once was a poor woman who had a cow.' It would be a wild paradox in modern England to imagine that a *poor* woman could have a cow; but things seem to have been different in ruder and more superstitious ages."[10]

Furthermore, Chesterton maintained that, besides being the only basis for justice, small proprietorship was the only social arrangement that had the weight of natural human emotion on its side. He drew attention to the social stability of peasant countries, and to the extreme tenacity with which small peasants from Ireland to Serbia or Poland clung to their little patch of land. Although no such class existed in England, having been virtually wiped out by the enclosures of the sixteenth to eighteenth centuries, he thought that he could nevertheless discern signs of similar feeling, in spite of the almost irresistible pressure of both capitalist monopoly and official social reform against it:

... we live in a time when it is harder for a free man to make a home than it was for a medieval ascetic to do without one.

The quarrel about the Limehouse slums was a working model of the problem. ... The slum dwellers actually and definitely say that they prefer their slums to the blocks of flats provided as a refuge from the slums. And they prefer them, it is stated, because the old homes had backyards in which they could pursue "their hobbies of bird-fancying and poultry-rearing." When offered other opportunities on some scheme of allotment, they had the hideous depravity to say that they liked fences round their private yards. So awful and overwhelming is the Red torrent of Communism as it boils through the brains of the working classes.[11]

Chesterton believed that the desire to possess one's own little domain, within which one could order things as one pleased, was so fundamental in human nature that if a policy of restoring property to ordinary men was once begun it would build up its own support. Such a policy would not have to fight against human inclinations with a mass of regulations and an army of inspectors, since ordinary emotions would rush to its support. What he had in mind was not some future Distributist utopia in which everyone was obliged to be a small proprietor, but rather a situation in which there were enough small proprietors to be a political force separate from both large-scale Capital and organized Labor, able to influence policy and legislation from their own standpoint.

What he and the other Distributists hoped to do, in fact, was to make England more like the rest of Europe and America. As he never ceased to point out, it was England and not the rest of the world that was out of step, in having no substantial class of peasants and small craftsmen. The vast bulk of modern Englishmen, and certainly of those who were politically active, were connected with industry in one way or another, whether as capitalists, proletarians, or employees; hence it was easy for them to dismiss the whole idea of small proprietorship as out-moded and anachronistic—just as Marx had called the peasants and petty bourgeoisie "transitional classes." But Chesterton had learned from Belloc to see English history and English problems within a wider European context, and to recognize the startling differences between England, with its almost entirely industrial society, and most of the European countries, with their large peasant populations.

Looking back at Chesterton now, from the standpoint of an even more irrevocably industrialized England, it is easy to exaggerate the absurdity of his dreams of a land of free peasants.

Yet during those years after World War I—when industrial societies were in a state of crisis everywhere, with inflation and depression causing successive havoc, and the richest countries suffering massive unemployment—the peasants in many parts of Europe wielded conscious political influence for the first, and perhaps the last, time. The Versailles settlement not only created new nation states out of the wreck of the Central European empires: it also gave votes to populations that were in many cases composed overwhelmingly of peasants.[12] For a while in the 1920s, before they were dislodged by right-wing coups d'état, peasant parties with large electoral majorities ruled most of the nations in Eastern Europe. The climax of this false dawn came in 1927 with the founding of the Green International, eventually joined by seventeen European peasant parties, though it collapsed as the 1930s ushered in the age of the dictators.

It is not surprising that Chesterton saw this rise of peasantries with a political voice as a hopeful sign for the future, and an indication that "progress" was not so inexorable as the English tended to suppose. Even in Britain the notion of small proprietorship was more feasible in the 1920s than it would be now. There were still substantial numbers of craftsmen and small businesses; the chain stores had only begun to swallow the small shops; and there was still a sufficiently large proportion of the population working on the land to make peasant proprietorship seem an important issue. The Liberal Party, indeed, had a long history of commitment to land reform of one sort or another, partly because of the hostility between landlords and tenants in the largely Liberal areas of rural Wales and Scotland. It is true that when Radicals attacked the great landowners—as Lloyd George frequently did in his speeches—they usually proposed semi-socialist measures of nationalization or land taxation, rather than the distribution of the land to a free peasantry. Yet one of the great radical electioneering slogans of the period, addressed to England agricultural laborers, was "Three Acres and a Cow."

All the same, however justifiable one might think Chesterton's views on property, and however reasonable it may have been to propound such views in the years after World War I, it is hard to deny that the Distributist movement was a sorry spectacle.

The Distributist League began largely as a by-product of *G.K.'s Weekly*. This paper was a reincarnation of the *New Witness,* the editorship of which Chesterton had taken over when his brother Cecil went off to fight and die in the war. In spite of the devoted readers that Chesterton could always attract, *G.K.'s Weekly,* like most small newspapers, was in perennial financial trouble, and it was partly in the hope of increasing its sales that a league was founded in 1926 to promote its principle of small property for all. At the inaugural meeting in London, Chesterton was elected president and enunciated the principles of the League in the words of Francis Bacon: "Property is like muck, it is good only if it be spread."

The League quickly gained a modest membership with branches all over the country, and for a time the sales of *G.K.'s Weekly* soared. However, it had no policy for action— there was, for instance, no question of putting up parliamentary candidates—and it quickly became a talking-shop for middle-class idealists, and split into warring factions after the classic manner of such bodies. There were quarrels over the financing of the paper, which was managed with deplorable inefficiency; there was ill feeling between Catholic and non-Catholic members; some of the more active idealists attempted to start agricultural settlements, with the usual disastrous failures; while those who stuck safely to talking at the League's meetings— which Chesterton rarely attended—found themselves deeply split over the place of machinery in a Distributist utopia. Some members were fanatical medievalists in homespun garments, who wished to dismantle industrial civilization lock, stock, and barrel; others opposed this, and furious passions arose over such issues as whether a dentist's drill was or was not a machine for the purposes of utopia.

It is clear that Chesterton himself found the whole affair

89

deeply embarrassing. As presiding genius and (absentee) editor of *G.K.'s Weekly,* he was appealed to by all factions and expected to arbitrate in all disputes; despite his considerable tact, it was impossible for him to satisfy everyone. But apart from the strain of having to be a universal peacemaker, his connection with the League put him into an unpleasantly false position, for the whole atmosphere of the League was at odds with his own philosophy.

To begin with, Chesterton had always appealed to and tried to speak for the common man, and had derided the crankiness of the vegetarian Socialists in their hygienic garments. But these could hardly be further from the common man than medievalist Catholic Distributists in homespun, even if the latter did drink beer. And then, the whole utopian cast of mind was alien to him. Back in 1905, in *Heretics,* he had already remarked, in words that could be used as a trenchant criticism of the Distributist disputes over machinery: "... the weakness of all Utopias is this, that they take the greatest difficulty of man and assume it to be overcome, and then give an elaborate account of the overcoming of the smaller ones."[13]

The truth is that much of Chesterton's social thought had the dangerous virtues that he was fond of attributing to orthodox Christianity: it was as a matter of fact sane and reasonable, but it lay only a hairsbreadth away from insanities of simplification, into which it was all too easy for heretics to topple. Instances of this can be found in his views on medievalism and on machinery. He often pointed out, for example, that the guild system of the Middle Ages was in some ways vastly superior to modern industrial organization. In that system of small tradesmen, the master was actually skilled in his craft, and was not merely a man with money; while the apprentice, though subject to a discipline that was often harsh, in the course of time had the chance of becoming a master himself. Furthermore, the guilds maintained a rough equality within the trade, prevented monopoly, and kept up standards of workmanship. In preferring this system to industrial capitalism, Chesterton was quite willing to call himself a medievalist: but he would have nothing to do with the escapist romanticism into which so many medievalists fell. In a criticism of William Morris, for instance,[14] he had pointed out that Morris's attempts to beautify everyday objects were directed toward preindustrial objects, and therefore touched the lives of ordinary people very little. If he had acted in that true medieval spirit that created gargoyles, he would have beautified such mundane things as railway signals.

Chesterton's discussion, in *The Outline of Sanity,* of the vexed question of machinery is entirely typical of his attitude. He did not share the hatred of the extreme Distributists for anything more complicated than a hand loom. On the contrary, he emphasized the fascination and romance of machinery, and its potentiality for increasing the power and independence of men. His quarrel with the modern world was simply that machinery was being used not to free men but to imprison them, to make their lives less interesting and more circumscribed than before. The important thing, therefore, was not to abolish machinery in a fury of iconoclasm, but to set it in its proper relation to human beings: "The best and shortest way of saying it is that instead of the machine being a giant to which the man is a pigmy, we must at least reverse the proportions until man is a giant to whom the machine is a toy."[15]

Insofar as modern inventions could actually help men to be independent and self-sufficient, Chesterton welcomed them. He would certainly have approved of intermediate technology, that is, the use of modern capabilities to help with traditional tasks such as peasant farming, in preference to sweeping away the whole of a traditional economic and social system in the name of modernization. The new Western ideal of the updated peasant, with his freezer stocked with home-grown vegetables, is very much in the Chesterton tradition.[16] He even had a certain qualified enthusiasm for the Ford car, just then in its heyday, simply because it was a small and private means of transport in which a man could go where he pleased, instead of being dependent upon the vast monopolistic organization of the railways. If he had lived to see the ravages of the motor car in modern conurbations, he would no doubt have changed his mind; but the point is rather that those conurbations are themselves a product of the drift toward larger and larger-scale organizations, against which he tried to fight.

His own Distributist writings are on the whole free from the utopianism of some of his associates, though they create problems of a different kind. In *The Outline of Sanity* he took great care to stress that Distributism was not just a dream of an ideal society, to be realized at some far-off future date. On the contrary, a start could be made here and now toward the restoration of small property, by means of various small and quite practicable steps. For instance, once shoppers fully realized that the defeat of small shops by chain stores was not an inexorable fate, they could choose deliberately to withdraw their custom from big shops and to patronize the small shops that remained, thus saving them and encouraging others. He suggested a number of changes in the law, none of them revolutionary, to aid the redistribution of property: for example, the replacement of primogeniture by the Napoleonic law, according to which inherited property is divided among the children. If a government were once to be converted by popular pressure toward encouraging small property instead of discouraging it, plenty of practical methods would be available to it, ranging from legal aid enabling small men to defend their little properties against the rich, to government subsidies aiding the establishment of small enterprises, and tariffs to protect them.[17] The obvious problem raised by such suggestions, however, was how to generate enough political pressure to secure this protection for a class of small proprietors that did not yet exist. From what source could Distributist reforms come?

One of Chesterton's allegorical fantasies, *Tales of the Long Bow,* describes an imaginary Distributist revolution, and brings out vividly the difficulty of relating Distributist dreams to practical politics. The book consists of a series of stories recounting the linked adventures of a group of eccentric English gentlemen, who contribute in a variety of ways to the re-establishment of a peasantry in England. Having done so, they lead the peasants to overthrow the governing clique of plutocrats and scientific cranks, who are bringing in socialistic measures as a means of perpetuating their own power. Among the many curious aspects of this literary extravaganza, two stand out. In the first place, the initial re-creation of small property in England is the work of a deus ex machina—an American millionaire who has been converted to Distributism by the heroes of the novel. Secondly these heroes, while acting on behalf of "the people," are thoroughly upper-class, old-style English gentlemen—whereas the plutocratic rulers of the country are portrayed as upstarts and aliens.

This fantasy of the creation of an ideal peasant republic through the chance association of a converted millionaire and a handful of right-minded gentry makes apparent the fundamental difficulty that Distributism presented for a populist like Chesterton: namely, its lack of popular support. By the time the Distributist movement was launched, no one could have supposed that it would have much appeal for the people whom Chesterton had most wanted to help—the casualties of industrialization. Indeed, as the League developed, it became clear that a substantial number of its supporters were distinctly right-wing in their attitudes, so that the support for the trade unions which Chesterton's paper expressed during the General Strike of 1926 angered many readers. In view of this, Chesterton's own relations with the labor movement demand more consideration.

Since antiindustrial movements like Distributism are often written off rather too easily as reactionary political phenomena, opposed to the cause of Labor, it is important to recognize Chesterton's unambiguous and often-declared sympathy with trade unions and strikers. At a time when the respectable classes usually regarded strikes as immoral and subversive—witness the enthusiasm with which middle-class volunteers opposed the General Strike—Chesterton continually defended industrial action. Indeed, he praised trade unions as the only modern institutions fit to be compared with the democratic guilds and communes of the Middle Ages, since they were the creation of ordinary working men. Before World War I—during the period of acute industrial conflict that was punctuated by the great strikes of miners, dockers, and railwaymen—he was emphatically with the Left of the labor movement on the strikers' side.[18]

His solidarity with striking workers did not, however, make him look with favor upon the various socialist and semisocialist schemes for state control or state intervention in industry. He was deeply suspicious of bureaucrats and professional politicians, and of those sprung from the ranks of the labor movement just as much as those with a longer official ancestry. Socialist or not, elected or not, such politicians seemed to him unrepresentative of the workmen for whom they claimed to speak, and in whose name they wished to exercise control of industry. He made his point eloquently in an essay sparked off by suggestions that industrial disputes might be dealt with by conciliation boards or compulsory arbitration courts on which Labor would be represented.[19] In a vivid (and unflattering) description, he evoked the common laborer of England—dirty, coarse in speech, not particularly sober. With this man he contrasted the sort of man to be found on any conceivable commission—clean, well-dressed, prosperous, educated—and pointed to the inevitable gulf between them, a gulf that fictions about representation could not cross.

The problem of how to apply Distributist principles to the large-scale industries in which so many of these laborers worked was not one that Chesterton ever discussed at length. However, in *The Outline of Sanity* he did indicate that he wished industries to belong to the workers—not in the fictitious sense of

94

public ownership exercised by civil servants, but in the direct sense that the workers should have disposable shares in their business, would have a shareholders' voice in company policy, and would divide the profits among themselves. He recognized that trade union opinion was deeply suspicious of profit-sharing schemes, which could be regarded as attempts on the part of the employers to buy industrial peace; but in spite of this, he concluded, "I think that profit-sharing that began at the popular end, establishing first the property of a guild and not merely the caprice of an employer, would not contradict any true principle of Trades Unions."[20]

Yet if it is true that, in a sense, the Distributist aim of property for all was theoretically compatible with the syndicalist aim of worker's ownership and control of industry, it is nevertheless obvious that the general drift of the British labor movement was away from small property and direct democracy, toward the extension of state control over economic and social life. In the heyday of British syndicalism, before World War I, a radical populist like Chesterton could without great incongruity write for a left-wing paper like the *Daily Herald;* but after the war the labor movement became much more solidly state-socialist in orientation.[21] Meanwhile the Russian Revolution gave rise to a new kind of Left, with which Chesterton had nothing in common; for if Fabian Socialism was not much more attractive to him than plutocratic capitalism, atheistic Bolshevik dictatorship on the Russian model was anathema.

Not that Chesterton had any objection to revolution as such. He constantly wrote as if a revolution of the poor against the rich were to be expected and welcomed, and he indulged himself with rhetorical references to storming the "fat white houses" in Park Lane.[22] Insofar as he did hope for a revolution, however, this underlines the most serious difficulty in his political thought —the problem of reconciling the revolutionary forces with which he sympathized with the result that he wished to achieve.[23] For there is no reason whatsoever to suppose that a revolution brought about by trade union leaders would have restored small property. That is to say, the popular movement with which he had most sympathy was incompatible with the kind of society he desired. Conversely, it cannot be claimed that the success of the Distributist movement would have been likely to help most factory workers. It might reasonably be argued, indeed, that insofar as a class of small property owners were created, the cause of property in general would have been greatly strengthened, and the remaining trade unions would have found themselves faced by an overwhelmingly hostile public opinion.

Chesterton never discussed this dilemma explicitly, but it emerges in allegorical form in the most interesting of his political novels, *The Return of Don Quixote*. This novel, which was appearing as a serial in *G.K.'s Weekly* at the time of the General Strike, has as one of its three heroes the militant syndicalist John Braintree, whose lack of rapport with the working man in the pub we observed in the last chapter. Braintree, the secretary of a miners' trade union, also organizes union activity among the workers employed on by-products of coal, and eventually masterminds a general strike. For the purposes of the (very improbable) plot, he occasionally appears at the local country house, and early in the novel silences his rich hosts with a marvelously eloquent speech about strikes. When one of those present mentions the unrest among the miners, Braintree points out the conception of a human being that is implied by calling it "peace" when that human being slaves away uninterruptedly, and "unrest" when he downs his tools:

"Suppose there is a man in your coal-cellar instead of your coal-mine. Suppose it is his business to break up coal all day, and you can hear him hammering. . . .

"The hammering in your coal-hole that always goes on stops for an instant. And what do you say to the man down there in the darkness? You do not say, 'Thank you for doing it well.' You do not even say, 'Damn you for doing it badly.' What you do say is, 'Rest; sleep on. Resume your normal state of repose. Continue in that state of complete quiescence which is natural to you and which nothing should ever have disturbed. Continue that rhythmic and lulling motion that must be to you the same as slumber. . . .'

"But the man in the coal-cellar is only a stranger out of the street," he went on, "who has gone into your black hole to attack a rock as he might attack a wild beast or any other brute force of nature. To break coal in a coal-cellar is an action. To break it in a coal-mine is an adventure. The wild beast can kill in its own cavern. . . .

"Don't you see," went on Braintree, "that when you say that of us, you imply that we are all so much clockwork, and you never notice the ticking till the clock stops."[24]

However, while Braintree, with his demands for workers' ownership and control of their industries, represents the most democratic side of the labor movement, he is not the only hero of the novel. He is balanced by Michael Herne, the idealistic ex-librarian who becomes the leader of a movement of romantic medievalism, dreaming of restoring the social order and pageantry of the Middle Ages. Although Herne eventually comes to the conclusion that syndicalism is a kind of modern reincarnation of the guild principle, his reactionary romanticism and idealized kingship have in the meantime been taken up and used cleverly by the aristocratic politicians, as a way of mobilizing propertied idealists in opposition to the labor movement—as a species of fascism, in fact. When, after a short reign as head of a new order of chivalry, Herne announces his discovery that medieval notions of social justice are on the side of the workers against the capitalists, he is of course dropped by his aristocratic backers; the net result of his career is that he becomes an outcast, a new Don Quixote who may perhaps occasionally right private injustice, but who can have no effect on politics. He retires into obscurity, accompanied by the novel's third major character. This is the ironic gentleman, Douglas Murrell, who is too wise to put any faith in political activity, and too detached and broad-minded to be capable of fanaticism on either side. Murrell, however, has himself already managed—by direct personal action—to rescue one victim of capitalist oppression and official tyranny: Dr. Hendry, the maker of fine paints.

The Return of Don Quixote is an extremely complex novel,[25] and its implications would seem to be threefold. In the first place, Chesterton claims that the spirit of medievalism which inspired so much of Distributism is not at all incompatible in theory with the syndicalist side of the labor movement, and that indeed the two ought to be standing together against plutocracy. Yet in the second place it is clear that, however true this may be in theory, in terms of practical politics the two are opposed; romantic reaction can all too easily be turned into a convenient tool *against* Labor, as in the case of fascism. The third implication seems to be that romantic medievalism, though illuminating in private life, is politically irrelevant if not dangerous: unless one can go along with the somewhat blinkered and narrow left-wing politics of Braintree, the only alternative is the sympathetic but apolitical detachment of Murrell, who understands the common people of England much better than the other two, but has no faith in or capacity for political action.

Chesterton never spelled out these implications, and the interpretation of the novel offered here is conjectural. Yet it is surely significant that a political novel published in 1927— just when he was beginning to campaign with the Distributist League—should have been so pessimistic, while in *Tales of the Long Bow,* published in 1925, he should have been more optimistic about Distributism only at the cost of shunning political realism completely. Some of the inertia and lack of forceful leadership with which certain Distributists reproached Chesterton[26] may have been due to an increasingly hopeless awareness— in spite of his public commitments—that the kind of society he desired was not a political possibility in England, since the people whom he had wished to help were enrolled under a different banner.

There is an interesting passage in one of Chesterton's prewar essays, in which meditations on a bonfire that burned down prematurely led him to think about revolutions:

And then I saw, in my vision, that just as there are two fires, so there are two revolutions. And I saw that the whole mad modern world is a race between them. Which will happen first—the revolution in which bad things shall perish, or that other revolution, in which good things shall perish also? One is the riot that all good men, even the most conservative, really dream of, when the sneer shall be struck from the face of the well-fed; when the wine of honour shall be poured down the throat of despair; when we shall, so far as to the sons of flesh is possible, take tyranny and usury and public treason and bind them into bundles and burn them. And the other is the disruption that may come prematurely, negatively, and suddenly in the night; like the fire in my little town.

It may come because the mere strain of modern life is unbearable; and in it even the things that men do desire may break down: marriage and fair ownership and worship and the mysterious worth of man. The two revolutions, white and black, are racing each other like two railway trains; I cannot guess the issue.[27]

To many people in the 1920s and 1930s there did indeed seem to be a confrontation between alternative revolutions— between Red and Black. Whether the revolution that Chesterton desired should be put in the same category as the black revolutions of fascism is a question to which we shall return in the next chapter. First, however, we shall look at another aspect of his thought that has considerable bearing on the question: his views on patriotism.

2. Nationalism and Notting Hill

... the patriot never under any circumstances boasts of the largeness of his country, but always, and of necessity, boasts of the smallness of it.[28]

Chesterton's version of patriotism, like so many of his opinions, was opposed to both the main controversial positions of the time. When he first worked out his own standpoint in the early 1900s, one of the great dividing lines in politics lay between the militant imperialists and the idealistic humanitarians. On one side stood those who believed that the British Empire represented the natural superiority of the Anglo-Saxon race, and that it had a sacred mission to conquer the world in the name of progress. Darwinian considerations strengthened the imperialists' faith, for their victories demonstrated their "fitness," while the inexorable laws of nature demanded that the weaker should go to the wall. Against the imperialists stood the motley and divided ranks of the humanitarians, many of them liberals or socialists, some of them adherents of the new Tolstoyan pacifism, but all of them agreed that the human race must progress beyond war toward universal brotherhood.

It was typical of Chesterton that he rejected both these positions. We have seen him and a few others take the Boer side in the South African war—not on pacifist and internationalist grounds, but on grounds of patriotism, claiming that a true English patriot must sympathize with the passionate loyalty of the Boers to their own small country. Some members of this pro-Boer group worked out their views in a volume entitled *England a Nation,* published in 1904,[29] to which Chesterton contributed the opening essay, "The Patriotic Idea." In this essay he directed his argument first against Tolstoyan pacifism, which had been received as a gospel by a good many English idealists. Chesterton argued in almost Burkean terms that love of humanity was empty unless it meant love above all of a specific, familiar section of humanity, in whose defense one must be prepared to fight. He denied categorically that patriotism, or indeed fighting, were evils in themselves: on the contrary, he maintained that, like love and wine, they were good things open to abuse.

The crux of his argument came, however, when he claimed that patriotism was menaced much less by pacifism than by imperialism. Imperialists treated the British Empire as an extension of the nation, and claimed patriotic loyalty in wars for Afghanistan or Zululand. But Chesterton insisted that this was to turn a genuine human emotion into an empty fiction: "If patriotism does not mean a defined and declared preference for certain traditions and surroundings, it means nothing whatever."[30] An empire on which the sun never sets is simply unimaginable, and cannot be the object of genuine patriotic emotion. As Chesterton recognized, the danger of very small commonwealths, like the city-states of the Middle Ages, is precisely the intensity of patriotic passion that they inspire. However, this did not seem to him the danger in his own time. In a world in which more and more of human experience was becoming second-hand and fictitious, he insisted that "we must at all costs get back to smaller political entities, because we must at all costs get back to reality."

He made this point more vividly in his celebrated novel, *The Napoleon of Notting Hill,* published in the same year as this essay. This is a fantasy about an England of the future which has apparently been strangled by bureaucracy, the machine running itself to such an extent that the King can be chosen at random from among the officials. At the beginning of the story, the royal dignity happens to fall upon a rather unusual official, Auberon Quinn, who is an irresponsible practical joker. Purely for his own amusement, he determines to re-create the London boroughs of Notting Hill, Bayswater, and the rest, and to endow them with medieval pageantry of his own design. He gets great fun out of seeing pompous civil servants and businessmen squirming in fantastic livery, and irritated by their statutory accompaniment of heralds and halberdiers.

However, the King's little joke is taken seriously by one man at least: the young Adam Wayne, who has grown up in Notting Hill, and whose love of its familiar streets blossoms into a fanatical attachment to the standard the King has set up. When the practical men at the heads of the neighboring boroughs propose a scheme for a new road that would involve knocking down a street in Notting Hill, Wayne opposes it; and when the businessmen and civil servants protest impatiently against letting trivial sentiment stand in the way of progress, he raises the farce to the level of epic through his own heroic seriousness:

"You have come, my Lord, about Pump Street?"

"About the city of Notting Hill," answered Wayne, proudly, "of which Pump Street is a living and rejoicing part."

"Not a very large part," said Barker, contemptuously.

"That which is large enough for the rich to covet," said Wayne, drawing up his head, "is large enough for the poor to defend."[31]

Wayne calls out the citizens of Notting Hill to defend their homes against the armed might of the rest of London; after fierce hand-to-hand street battles with ancient weapons, he at last brings off a coup by capturing the water tower on Campden Hill and threatening to flood his enemies unless they surrender. But Wayne has not only succeeded in winning the battle: he has also inspired in his enemies his own passionate patriotism. The once-prosaic businessmen and officials of the other boroughs are now patriots and soldiers as well, and when Notting Hill in her triumph becomes arrogant they rise against her. Wayne falls gloriously in the last battle.

In *The Napoleon of Notting Hill* one can discern the two strands that together make up Chesterton's attitude to patriotism, and that may well induce ambivalent feelings in his readers. On the one hand he evokes vividly the real stuff of human loyalties; on the other, his romanticism of violence is as cruelly unreal as Sorel's.

His first point—a powerful one—was that all the grand, large-scale, progressive intellectual movements of his time ignored the human emotions and the power of small local loyalties. He himself seems to have felt from childhood a passionate attachment to his own area of London, and he told a friend later how the first idea for *The Napoleon of Notting Hill* had come to him. He had begun conventionally, by sympathizing with the progressive and humanitarian intellectuals of his day, such as Shaw and Wells. But then:

I grew uneasily conscious that some of the things that they wanted to destroy were those which I wanted most to preserve. Little things; Neighbourly things. . . .

It came to me in a flash when I was walking down a certain street in Notting Hill. There was a row of shops. At one end was a public-house; somewhere at the farther end I rather think there was a church. And on the way there was a grocer's, there was a second-hand bookshop, there was an old curiosity shop where they sold, among other things, arms. There were, in fact, shops supplying all the spiritual and bodily needs of man.

All at once I realised how completely lost this bit of Notting Hill was in the modern world. It was asked to be interested in the endow-ment of a public library in Kamschatka by an American millionaire, or a war between an oil trust and another oil trust in Papua, or the splendid merger of all the grocery interests in Europe and America or the struggles between the brewers and the Prohibitionists to give us worse beer or less beer.

In all these world-shaking events this little bit of Notting Hill was of no account. And that seemed idiotic. For to this bit of Notting Hill the bit was of supreme importance.

In the same instant I saw that my Progressive friends were more bent than any on destroying Notting Hill. Shaw and Wells and the rest of them were interested only in world-shaking and world-making events. When they said, "Every day in every way better and better," they meant every day bigger and bigger—in every way. . . .

In that half-second of time, gazing with rapt admiration at the row of little shops, nobly flanked by a small pub and a small church, I discovered that not only was I against the plutocrats, I was against the idealists. . . . And, once for all, I drew my sword—purchased in the old curiosity shop—in defence of Notting Hill.[32]

As a result of ignoring such basic local loyalties, the large-scale thinkers—whether imperialist or idealist—seemed to Chesterton to find themselves out of touch with the real roots of popular politics. The imperialists had thought of the Boers as a small group of backward farmers who could be easily absorbed into the Empire, and had been severely shaken by the furious and tenacious resistance they put up. Attempts to govern Ireland, whether by coercion or conciliation, continually foundered, because British politicians of both parties seemed unable to realize that the Irish were a nation, wanting independence and not just reform.

If Chesterton's patriotism was opposed to any ideal of world-wide empire, it was just as strongly opposed to the fashionable belief in race and in determining racial characteristics. According to the prevalent anthropological theory of the time, the Teutons, Celts, and others were supposed to have different racial characteristics that were evident in their appearance, behavior, and political institutions. In view of the provenance of the doctrine, it is not surprising that the Teutons were regarded as the naturally superior race. Before solid German industry and German battleships began to seem more of a menace than Latin instability, it was common for pro-German politicians to talk of England, Germany, America, and the white Dominions as forming a natural community of blood, and having a joint responsibility for civilization. The strength of this climate of opinion can be judged from the fact that even Chesterton himself, in his youth, wrote a poem influenced by it.[33]

He quickly outgrew this youthful conformism, however, and thereafter poured undiluted scorn upon the racial theory. As he pointed out, the supposed characteristics of Teuton and Celt were being used to account for everything from the British Constitution to Irish jokes, while all the time no one could actually define or produce a Teuton or a Celt: "They first treat a Celt as an axiom and then treat an Irishman as an inference."[34] What was in fact real, solid, and observable was the nation—for instance, the Irish nation—with its national characteristics. Theories of race were attempts at materialistic explanations that in fact explained nothing. A nation is a real entity whose existence politicians ignore at their peril, but its reality is spiritual rather than physical—a matter of shared ideas, traditions, and loyalties, rather than anything as material as common blood:

The truth of the whole matter is very simple. Nationality exists, and has nothing in the world to do with race. Nationality is a thing like a church or a secret society; it is a product of the human soul and will; it is a spiritual product. And there are men in the modern world who would think anything and do anything rather than admit that anything could be a spiritual product.[35]

Precisely because a nation is a spiritual entity, there can be nothing fixed or inevitable about the size or nature of the unit of patriotism. When Chesterton pointed to examples of patriotism in his day, he turned naturally to nations on a fairly large scale, like France or Ireland or Poland. But in *The Napoleon of Notting Hill* he had underlined the possibility that the commonwealths for which men would die might be much smaller than that, as they had been among the city-states of medieval Italy and ancient Greece. This is a valid point, though it leads to an indeterminacy that eventually undermines his own theory of patriotism.

There is a particularly acute discussion of the idea of a nation in the travel book that Chesterton published after visiting America. He began by remarking that "travel narrows the mind": in spite of the universality of human nature, and the real spiritual possibility of human brotherhood, what strikes the traveler in a foreign land is how grotesquely different foreigners are. He suggested two principles with which to approach any foreign country: "The first principle is that nobody should be ashamed of thinking a thing funny because it is foreign: the second is that he should be ashamed of thinking it wrong because it is funny."[36] It is important first to recognize the real (and often grotesque) differences between nations, as a necessary preliminary for coming to understand them. For instance, Chesterton quoted the preposterous passport form he had been asked to fill out at the American consulate, including questions like "Are you an anarchist?" and "Are you in favor of subverting the government of the United States by force?" He felt free to laugh, but then went on to explain this (at the time) unique concern with the private beliefs of visitors, by pointing out that "America is the only nation in the world that is founded on a creed."[37] Because America took in all sorts of people and made them into Americans, what they believed might be a perfectly serious matter of concern (although a questionnaire might not seem a very efficient way of eliciting such information); whereas in an old, established nation like England, full of recognizable national types, it was much easier to judge what a particular man might or might not do: ". . . because we know his habits, we do not care about his opinions."[38]

Chesterton poured scorn on the facile notion, dear to journalists, that modern transport and communications were "bringing nations closer together." He pointed out that many of the most bitterly fought wars in human history had been waged between little states that were far too close together for comfort. If international friendship were to flourish, it would not do so because men were growing technologically closer or economically and socially similar: it would do so only insofar as they recognized and respected one another's real differences.

He himself not only insisted on these national differences but rejoiced in them: the cosmopolitanism of the time seemed to him quite misguided. One of the characters in *The Napoleon of Notting Hill* is a Nicaraguan patriot who has been defeated in a last-ditch struggle for his little country's independence. The English civil servants he talks to try to explain tactfully why they are unable to sympathize with Nicaraguan aspirations:

"We moderns believe in a great cosmopolitan civilization, one which shall include all the talents of the absorbed peoples—"

"The Senor will forgive me," said the President. "May I ask the Senor how, under ordinary circumstances, he catches a wild horse?"

"I never catch a wild horse," replied Barker, with dignity.

"Precisely," said the other; "and there ends your absorption of the talents. That is what I complain of in your cosmopolitanism. When you say you want all peoples to unite, you really mean that you want all peoples to unite to learn the tricks of your people. If the Bedouin Arab does not know how to read, some English missionary or schoolmaster must be sent to teach him to read, but no-one ever says, 'This schoolmaster does not know how to ride on a camel; let us pay a Bedouin to teach him.' You say your civilisation will include all the talents. Will it? Do you really mean to say that at the moment when the Esquimaux has learnt to vote for a County Council, you will have learnt to spear a walrus? I recur to the example I gave. In Nicaragua we had a way of catching wild horses—by lasooing the fore feet—which was supposed to be the best in South America. If you are going to include all the talents, go and do it. If not, permit me to say what I have always said, that something went from the world when Nicaragua was civilised."[39]

Indeed, as Chesterton often pointed out, the example of Ireland was sufficient disproof of this fallacy that the conqueror learns from the countries he absorbs. England had singularly failed to learn anything from or about Ireland, for English relations with Ireland had been ruined by a blindness born of contempt for the defeated.

The evils of cosmopolitanism seemed to him to be exemplified in the Indian nationalist movement of his time, on which he wrote an article that is said to have decisively influenced Gandhi.

The principal weakness of Indian Nationalism seems to be that it is not very Indian and not very national. . . .

Suppose an Indian said: "I heartily wish India had always been free from white men in all their works. Every system has its sins: and we prefer our own. There would have been dynastic wars; but I prefer dying in battle to dying in hospital. There would have been despotism; but I prefer one king whom I hardly ever see to a hundred kings regulating my diet and my children. . . . If you do not like our sort of spiritual comfort, we never asked you to. Go, and leave us with it." Suppose an Indian said that, I should call him an Indian Nationalist, or, at least, an authentic Indian, and I think it would be hard to answer him. But the Indian Nationalists whose words I have read simply say with ever-increasing excitability, "Give me a ballot-box. Provide me with a Ministerial dispatch-box. Hand me over the Lord Chancellor's wig. I have a natural right to be Prime Minister. I have a heaven-born claim to introduce a budget. My soul is starved if I am excluded from the Editorship of the *Daily Mail*"; or words to that effect.[40]

We have looked at the more attractive and plausible side of Chesterton's patriotism: his stress on the human inclination to be loyal to nations and commonwealths, which are spiritual and not material entities, but nonetheless real for all that. But the other aspect—equally clear in *The Napoleon of Notting Hill* and in many of Chesterton's writings—may well seem more questionable. This is his romanticism about fighting. It is clear that patriotism, or indeed any kind of political principle, generally does entail a willingness to fight as a last resort: but there is a difference—whether important or not—between the grim willingness to take up arms if absolutely necessary, and Chesterton's positive delight in the idea of battles and barricades. True, his militarism is of a generous kind, above all celebrating heroic hand-to-hand encounters. It has none of the vulgarity of those who bow down before big guns and battleships. Still less did he idolize conquerors: he remained explicitly within the epic tradition, where death in the face of overwhelming odds is especially glorious.

Like others of his generation who celebrated fighting, Chesterton was of course reacting against the pacifist and cosmopolitan ideals fashionable at the time, and he may have deliberately overstated his case. However, according to his brother, "he was not in the least averse either to violence or to bloodshed in themselves,"[41] while as an adult he was famous for playing constantly with swords and pistols. What really rings false to a reader now is the utter disparity between his swordplay, or his epic of heroic fighting in the streets of London, and that nightmare of guns, gas, barbed wire, and trenches that he justified in the name of patriotism. It is to his views of World War I that we must now turn.

Chesterton spent several months during the early part of the war in a coma, suffering the most severe illness of his life, and he was a long time recovering his strength. However, there could never have been any question of his going personally to fight, for he was totally unfit and gigantically fat. (There is a story of his being accosted one day in Fleet Street by a girl handing out white feathers to noncombatants. When she challenged him shrilly, "Why aren't you out at the front?" Chesterton is said to have replied, "My dear madam, if you will step round this way a little you will see that I *am*.") However, it seems reasonable to suppose that his own inability to fight may have contributed to the fanaticism of the propaganda pamphlets that were his own war work. In the first, *The Barbarism of Berlin,* published in 1914, he maintained that the Kaiser's broken pledge to respect Belgian neutrality was entirely typical of Prussian immorality. The Germans, he said, were barbarians in a far more serious sense than the Russians—England's allies, to the embarrassment of many liberals—for they refused to recognize the principle of reciprocal obligation upon which all morality was founded, and acted as if laws did not apply to them. He went so far as to claim that the brutal Prussian attitude to power could be seen in the fact that Prussian men sat down while their wives stood.

The Crimes of England, published in 1915, is even worse. In it he argued that England had erred in helping to bring about the rise of Prussia in the eighteenth and nineteenth centuries, when her proper place should have been by the side of the Christian and democratic French. This view of history, which turns up frequently in Chesterton's works, shows the influence of Hilaire Belloc. Belloc and Chesterton spent a good deal of energy trying to correct the traditional English identification with Northern, Germanic, Protestant Europe, affirming instead that the Mediterranean countries were the true heirs of Christian and Catholic civilization.

Chesterton's fullest statement of this position occurs in his book on Fascist Italy, *The Resurrection of Rome,* which will be treated more fully later. Early in the book he considered the various theories that had been put forward about the underlying causes of World War I, and rejected them all in favor of one shared, he admitted, by no one except Cecil Chesterton and Belloc. The basic thesis was that, until the war, power and authority in Europe had been topsy-turvy. The stereotype of the low "dago" symbolized the extent to which, in the cult of Nordic nations, the Latin origins of European civilization had been forgotten. According to this theory, the underlying rationale of the war was the need to correct this imbalance: "It was this feeling of reaction against the *nouveau riche* of Europe, against the Prussian parvenu and his like, when they looked down on the Latin culture, which was the deepest driving force of the Great War . . . it was . . . in the last resort simply Rome shaking off the barbarians."[42]

This view is eccentric, to say the least, and it is hard not to feel that Chesterton was out of his depth in trying to explain the catastrophic international politics of his time. What is particularly disquieting about his writings on the war, however, is the apparent elasticity of his conception of patriotism. At its most intelligible and appealing, patriotism as he describes it is the defense of a small city against overwhelming forces. The difficulty is to connect this with a world war in which England was fighting along with a motley collection of allies, not for her own frontiers, but at Jerusalem and Gallipoli as well as in France. If imperialism could be denounced as an unreal extension of fictitious patriotism, why did not the same apply to the cause of the Allies?

Chesterton would probably have answered that World War I was a crusade in defense of civilization against barbarism, and could have quoted, as evidence of his own consistency, Adam Wayne's dictum that "there were never any just wars but the religious wars."[43] But the difficulty is that crusades are all too common. Imperialists in South Africa at the turn of the century; both fascists and Communists in Spain in the 1930s; Americans and their enemies in Vietnam—all have been too easily convinced that their war was a crusade. It is unfortunately true that people fight just as readily and with quite as much fanaticism for purely imaginary causes, as they do for the solid walls of their father's house. Chesterton's romantic defense of local patriotism, which seemed as if it might provide some criterion for determining when war is justified, slides too easily into a defense of world war to be helpful. All it does, in the last resort, is cast a spurious glamor over the horror of the trenches.

5

The Ball and the Cross

1. Christianity and the Epic Tradition

> I tell you naught for your comfort,
> Yea, naught for your desire,
> Save that the sky grows darker yet
> And the sea rises higher.
>
> Night shall be thrice night over you,
> And heaven an iron cope.
> Do you have joy without a cause,
> Yea, faith without a hope?[1]

The *Ballad of the White Horse,* which was much quoted in England in the dark days of the Battle of Britain in 1940, was Chesterton's longest and most ambitious poem. It is about King Alfred's fight against the Danish conquest of England, and it might at first sight be regarded as a piece of medievalist romanticism. But Chesterton saw its theme as intensely relevant to his own day. Alfred was for him a symbol of the power of quite ordinary men, when sustained by Christian faith, to fight heroically and untiringly against overwhelming odds. In that England of the Dark Ages the tide of history was running strongly in favor of the Norse invaders. These heathen plunderers of monasteries represented the future, and might be regarded as the most "progressive" forces of their time. Since they undoubtedly survived more efficiently than the Christians, they were presumably "fitter" in evolutionary terms; indeed, their brutal and overwhelming energy gave them a marked resemblance to late nineteenth-century visions of the superman. But Alfred and the little bands of Christians he rallied did not accept the judgment of history or bow down to the forces of the future. Instead they fought, and when defeated, regrouped and fought again—with no chance of final victory, but with a heroism that at last achieved a transfiguring compromise when the conquering Danes agreed to adopt Christianity.

In this story from the remote past Chesterton found a much-needed moral for his own time. It seemed to him that the contemporary loss of Christian faith was not only an individual calamity, but a political and social one. The vacuum left by the loss of Christian ideals was being filled, in one form or another, by the blind worship of historical inevitability. "Progress," he remarked, "is Providence without God."[2]

When Chesterton's brother Cecil published an anonymous critique of his writings in 1908,[3] he made much of the amazing fact that this paradoxical new thinker did not believe in Progress. At the time, almost everyone else in intellectual circles did, in one form or another. There was still a good deal of life left in the liberal doctrine, according to which science and enlightenment were gradually triumphing over superstition and ignorance: indeed, the history of England was usually described in corresponding terms, with the Reformation and the 1688 Revolution as the chief signposts along the road from barbarism to civilization. But upon this liberal doctrine had been superimposed various specifically nineteenth-century versions of progress, ranging from evolutionary theories of the ultimate dominance of a race of supermen to more or less Marxist theories of inevitable revolution. Even the new pessimists, who believed that Western civilization was sliding into decadence, drew their conclusions with a gloomy quietism and did not feel called upon to do anything to stop the decline. Intellectuals in the early years of the century differed about many things, but what they almost all had in common was the sense of living on an escalator of historical forces that was taking them willy-nilly toward the future. The notion that anyone might jump off the escalator or try to put it into reverse was a very startling heresy.

Chesterton drew attention to many examples of this sense of inevitability, or, as he sometimes called it, "impenitence." "We are subconsciously dominated in all departments by the notion that there is no turning back, and it is rooted in materialism and the denial of free will."[4] Even the men of action were paralyzed by this sense that the stream of history was irreversible. Chesterton compared the English kings of the Middle Ages, who had tried again and again to reverse the decision of history, and to regain their lost territories in France, with the supposedly tough-minded imperialists of his own age, who never dreamed for a moment of trying to reconquer America.

The sense of floating helplessly upon the inevitable stream of history seemed to Chesterton particularly characteristic of attitudes toward machinery and technological innovation. He examined such notions mercilessly in a chapter of *The Outline of Sanity* entitled "The Wheel of Fate": "What is precisely meant by the statement that the steam-engine or the wireless apparatus has come to stay?"[5] Men have become so mesmerized by such phrases that they forget they are themselves creators. However, people in Paris in the eighteenth century no doubt said that the Bastille had come to stay. "But it did not stay; it left the neighborhood quite abruptly. In plain words, the Bastille was something that man had made and, therefore, man could unmake."[6] It seemed vital to Chesterton to reassert human sovereignty over the things that man has made. For technological progress was not an end in itself, still less an inexorable fate: it was a matter of human inventions that are worth keeping if they serve human happiness, but that should be scrapped if they do not.

The aim of human policy is human happiness. . . . There is no law of logic or nature or anything else forcing us to prefer anything else. There is no obligation on us to be richer, or busier, or more efficient, or more productive, or more progressive, or in any way worldlier or wealthier, if it does not make us happier. Mankind has as much right to scrap its machinery and live on the land, if it really likes it better, as any man has to sell his old bicycle and go for a walk, if he likes that better. It is obvious that the walk will be slower; but he has no duty to be fast.[7]

Where this belief in inevitability was concerned, Chesterton saw little to choose among his contemporaries: Socialist revolutionaries, for instance, were just as bad as imperialists or worshippers of technological progress. He remarked in his *Autobiography* that the Socialists he knew never seemed to expect that they would have to *fight* for their revolution: they envisaged it as coming inexorably and of its own accord. Even their revolutionary songs were not songs of struggle, but were about waiting for the dawn.

... the English revolutionary poet wrote as if he owned the sun and was certain to be the conqueror. In other words, I found that the Socialist idea of war was exactly like the Imperialist idea of war; and I was strengthened and deepened in my detestation of both of them. I heard many arguments against the idea of a Class War; but the argument which discredits it for me is the fact that the Socialists, like the Imperialists, always assumed that they would win the war. I am no Fascist; but the March on Rome gave them the surprise they needed. To say the least, it considerably halted the inevitable proletarian triumph; just as the Boers had halted the inevitable British triumph. And I do not like inevitable triumphs.[8]

Chesterton thought this belief in inevitability unrealistic and damaging, for a number of reasons. In the first place, those who held it were denying human powers and evading human responsibilities. Against this prevailing consensus he emphatically reasserted human freedom:

There is one metaphor of which the moderns are very fond; they are always saying, 'You can't put the clock back.' The simple and obvious answer is, 'You can.' A clock, being a piece of human construction, can be restored by the human finger to any figure or hour.

In the same way society, being a piece of human construction, can be reconstructed upon any plan that has ever existed.[9]

All the time, men were in fact transforming the world by their actions, yet they refused to recognize that they had the power to make choices about the ways in which they transformed it. Instead, they simply followed the strongest tendency and drifted with the stream.

Worse than this mere spinelessness was what seemed to follow from it—the quite immoral cult of success: the assumption that the strongest tendency must be the right one, that the dominant nation or social system must be the best, that the losers in history must be wrong. As Chesterton remarked, the modern world was on the side of the Giant against Jack: it was prepared to accept any conqueror as a superman, and had apparently forgotten all about the epic tradition, with its celebration of the lone hero or the small band of men struggling desperately against overwhelming odds.

Chesterton attributed this loss of moral courage and this blind acceptance of fate to modern irreligion. He made the point squarely in his early book, *Heretics,* in which he took to task some of the most celebrated writers of the time for their "heresies"—that is, the deficiencies in their philosophies of life. In a chapter entitled "On the Negative Spirit," he pointed out that modern intellectuals were paralyzed by their lack of definite ideals.

Every one of the popular modern phrases and ideals is a dodge in order to shirk the problem of what is good. . . . The modern man says, "Let us leave all these arbitrary standards and embrace liberty." This is, logically rendered, "Let us not decide what is good, but let it be considered good not to decide it." He says, "Away with your old moral formulae; I am for progress." This, logically stated, means, "Let us not settle what is good; but let us settle whether we are getting more of it." He says, "Neither in religion nor morality, my friend, lie the hopes of the race, but in education." This, clearly expressed, means, "We cannot decide what is good, but let us give it to our children."[10]

The paralyzed acceptance of historical inevitability, the worship of a quite pointless "progress" and a quite empty "efficiency" were, according to Chesterton, merely attempts to disguise the moral vacuum at the heart of modern thought. Lacking genuine ideals, intellectuals took up the latest fashion in opinions just as they followed the fashion in their clothes; or else they adopted a stance of openness to any idea from any source, in the vague hope that good would come of it. As Chesterton remarked of H. G. Wells, "I think he thought that the object of opening the mind is simply opening the mind. Whereas I am incurably convinced that the object of opening the mind, as of opening the mouth, is to shut it again on something solid."[11]

Faced with this impotent agnosticism, Chesterton never ceased to insist that only a sure faith in an ideal can enable a man to achieve anything. Men can stand against the tide of history and defy the dominant trends of the time, as Alfred did: but only if, as in Alfred's case, their heroism is sustained by faith in a definite ideal. Certainly Chesterton's own ability to question the trends of his time and to champion unfashionable and "reactionary" causes was closely bound up with his own religion; we must now consider to what extent he should be regarded as a purely Christian or Catholic thinker.

Ever since the latter part of his life, Chesterton has often been lumped together with Belloc as a Roman Catholic writer, his writings seen as propaganda for the Church of Rome, and his political ideas as typically Roman Catholic. It is certainly understandable that Roman Catholics in England should have been eager to claim such a prestigious convert. However, it is important to remember that, unlike Belloc, Chesterton was not Catholic by origin or upbringing. After growing up in a liberal Protestant household he became an Anglo-Catholic, remained an Anglican for many years, and joined the Roman Catholic Church only in 1922. In other words, his views were formed long before he became a Roman Catholic, and there could never have been any question of his having learned his characteristic ways of thought from the Church. In the early years of the century, when he was castigating "heretics" and proclaiming "orthodoxy," he was being consciously paradoxical, for at the time he represented no one but himself. He was certainly Christian in his views from the time that he first began to write: but it is much more doubtful whether his thought can be called Roman Catholic.

To be sure, there is considerable ambiguity about what are specifically Roman Catholic—let alone Christian—views on many questions. For instance, a caricature of Roman Catholic political views—with a good deal of European evidence to support it—would emphasize authority, hierarchy, and obedience, and the Church's opposition to freedom, equality, and revolution. It is obvious that Chesterton had nothing in common with that kind of traditional right-wing Catholicism. However, quite opposite notions can also be found in Catholic traditions, particularly in the Thomist tradition revived in the late nineteenth century: notions of natural law; of popular sovereignty and the right to resist bad governments; of limits on riches, and concern for the poor. Leo XIII's encyclical *Rerum Novarum,* promulgated in 1891, showed a sympathy with the working class and a desire for more equal division of property that derived from this Thomist tradition. While the tone of such Papal pronouncements remained cautious and conservative, there was much in them that could be taken up by radical Catholics and readily reconciled with Chesterton's Distributism.

Chesterton did not derive his political views from the authority of the Church. On the other hand, as he articulated his views and became fully aware of them, he became convinced both that they were intrinsically dependent upon Christianity, and that the salient doctrines of Christianity were best represented within the Roman Catholic Church. He stated his position most clearly in a late work, *The Thing* (1929), where he said that "the modern world, with its modern movements, is living on its Catholic capital."[12] Insofar as modern men still had any political ideals, these were Christian ideals; and insofar as they became detached from a genuine Christian faith, they withered away. Chesterton argued, in fact, that all the principles of the French Revolution and of modern reform movements—the creed of liberty, equality, and fraternity, together with faith in the possibility of heroic action to make the world better—were all derived from Christianity, and could not long survive away from it.

This point seemed most obvious in the case of the political principle dearest to Chesterton's heart—equality. He remarked that to his own generation of liberal and enlightened ex-Christians, growing up at the end of the nineteenth century, the equal worth of all human beings had seemed an obvious truth that did not need religious mythology about the Fatherhood of God to back it up. But in his own lifetime he watched the spread of doctrines dividing men into superior and inferior races, or elites and masses, and was convinced that "there is no basis for democracy except in a dogma about the divine origin of man."[13] Changes in prevailing American views on the black population illustrated the point. The Founding Fathers, recognizing the common nature of all men, regarded slavery as a *problem:* but Darwinism and racial theory rapidly convinced nineteenth-century Southerners that there was no moral problem at all, for blacks were not really human. Only Christian dogma, upheld by a Church that ordained black priests, could stand against this inhuman tide of the time.

Darwinism in the late nineteenth century was very much more than a scientific hypothesis. It was an antireligious creed which seemed to Chesterton to carry profound and dangerous moral implications. He felt some sympathy with the American opponents of Darwinism (who included the old Populist, William Jennings Bryan) and explained why in an essay entitled "The Evolution of Slaves."[14] He had, he said, heard a clever young American defending prohibition on the grounds that it could not be regarded as a violation of liberty, since future generations reared under its sway would not feel any desire for drink. And it was this notion, that the nature of man is plastic and open to modification for the sake of social convenience, that seemed to him dangerously immoral.

When my young American friend talked of the next generation growing up without the desire for "alcohol," he had at the back of his mind a certain idea. It is the idea which I have just seen expressed by another American in a high-brow article, in the words: "Evolution does not stand still. We are not finished. The world is not finished." What it means is that the nature of man can be modified to suit the convenience of particular men; and this would certainly be very convenient. If the rich man wants the miners to live underground, he may really breed for it a new race as blind as bats and owls.[15]

The modern loss of Christianity, therefore, and particularly its replacement by Darwinism, seemed to Chesterton to open up totalitarian possibilities. But even at a more immediate and less nightmarish level, unbelief was insidiously destructive of human equality. Chesterton stressed the ways in which the Church, in the days of its strength, stood against worldly criteria of superiority and inferiority. In the absence of Christian principles, some are revered because they are strong or clever or handsome, or above all because they are rich and powerful. But a saint was simply a man who was *good,* and that could be anyone, no matter how poor or humble or stupid. The complement of the Christian doctrine that anyone, however humble, can become a saint, is the doctrine of Original Sin—that everyone, however highly placed, is a sinner and can be called to account. In his *Short History of England* Chesterton reflected on the amazing fact that Henry II was publicly scourged in Canterbury Cathedral after authorizing the murder of Becket.

If the reader can imagine Mr. Cecil Rhodes submitting to be horse-whipped by a Boer in St. Paul's Cathedral, as an apology for some indefensible death incidental to the Jameson Raid, he will form but a faint idea of what was meant when Henry II was beaten by monks at the tomb of his vassal and enemy.[16]

Without a firm religious backing for the doctrine of human equality, Chesterton saw nothing to stop the natural drift toward praising the successful for their success and stigmatizing the poor as unfit and inferior.

If equality was the most obvious case where an apparently secular political ideal relied on religious dogma, the principle of liberty seemed to Chesterton equally vulnerable to erosion by unbelief. One of the great materialist orthodoxies of the time was the belief in determinism and denial of free will. This belief was in many cases held by humanitarians who were opposed to what seemed to them bloodthirsty notions of retribution; but its implications, as Chesterton pointed out, were far from humane. In his essay "The Mercy of Mr. Arnold Bennett," he pointed out that the danger of refusing to judge people is that it involves not only denying man's responsibility and dignity, but also refusing to distinguish between the guilty and the innocent.

The logical process through which the discussion passes is always the same; I have seen it in a hundred debates about fate and free-will. First someone says, like Mr. Bennett: "Let us be kinder to our brethren, and not blame them for faults we cannot judge." Then some casual commonsense person says: "Do you really mean you would let anybody pick your pocket or cut your throat without protest?" Then the first man always answers as Mr. Bennett does: "Oh no; I would punish him to protect myself and protect society; but I would not *blame* him, because I would not venture to judge him."[17]

Chesterton remarked that to punish people but not blame them is actually less considerate to the individual than the older position. Punishing a man purely for the protection of society implies no regard for him as a man at all, nor any sense of the appropriate limits of the punishment. ". . . in heathen Rome . . . it was a common practice to torture the slaves of any household subjected to legal enquiry. If you had remonstrated, because no crime had been proved against the slaves, the State would have answered in the modern manner: 'We are not punishing the crime; we are protecting the community.' "[18] This parallel did not seem far-fetched to Chesterton, since the class upon whom the weight of "protecting society" would fall was certainly the poor. Already in England some poor people were being tortured by having their children taken from them on eugenic grounds, because they had been classified as defective. "Nobody could pretend that the affectionate mother of a rather backward child *deserves* to be punished by having all the happiness taken out of her life. But anybody can pretend that the act is needed for the happiness of the community."[19]

The loss of Christian faith seemed to Chesterton to lead insidiously, through devious routes of well-intentioned ideas, to the denial of human equality, the denial of human freedom, and the belief that men are helpless victims of fate. This seemed to him a disastrous travesty of the human situation. For him men were immortal souls, each of them a priceless individual who was the center of his own world, each capable of making earth-shaking choices and changing the course of history. This view of humanity seemed to him to be borne out by experience: as he remarked in *The Napoleon of Notting Hill,* the human race enjoyed playing the game of "Cheat the Prophet," and disproving all the predictions made by the wise men of the previous generation. But this obvious common-sense view of the human condition was in fact preserved only within dogmatic Christianity that had not succumbed to modernist influence—the Roman Catholic Church, in fact—and was denied by all the "progressive" thought of the day.

The period in which Chesterton grew up was a great age of ersatz religions, ranging from esoteric cults vaguely derived from the East to humanitarian creeds so formless that there was nothing they excluded. Particularly common among well-meaning English intellectuals was the view that true Christianity had nothing to do with dogma, and this Chesterton continually attacked. One of the chief intellectual faults of his time seemed to him to be an all-pervading wooliness of mind, which allowed people to drift into accepting principles that they would never have sanctioned if they had clearly considered their implications. Christian belief meant to Chesterton not the sort of vague humanitarian emotion of which there was abundance, but a clarity of principle and conviction that was sadly lacking. This clarity he eventually believed he had found in the Roman Catholic Church.

Nevertheless there is a certain irony here, for the authoritative doctrine that the Church taught turned out to have a curiously Chestertonian flavor. Catholic theology and Catholic traditions include a medley of different strands, notably the rivalry between Augustinian and Thomistic theology. The perfectly genuine Catholic traditions of more-than-puritan asceticism, and of authoritarian demands for submission, found no echo in Chesterton's thought, whereas in his hands Thomism turned into a populist philosophy of sanity and common sense.

In 1933, only three years before his death, Chesterton published a remarkable popular study of Thomas Aquinas. He began the book with a comparison between Saint Thomas and Saint Francis of Assisi, on whom he had already written, and asserted that "they both reaffirmed the Incarnation, by bringing God back to earth."[20] Saint Francis had established a peculiarly Christian form of asceticism, one which was able to practice rigid self-denial while at the same time loving and affirming creation. Similarly, Saint Thomas had established a peculiarly Christian form of rationalism, which, in contrast to the Platonism previously fashionable, laid great stress on ordinary human experience and the evidence of the senses. Chesterton's point was that "these men became more orthodox, when they became more rational or natural."[21]

What Chesterton was in fact doing was to present the Catholic Church and its central Thomistic theological tradition as the guardian of sanity and common sense, against the coherent but unbalanced heresies to which unaided intellect is continually attracted. He pointed out that most of the really brilliant philosophies that have been constructed actually contradict human experience, instead of accounting for it: "Since the modern world began in the sixteenth century, nobody's system of philosophy has really corresponded to everybody's sense of reality; to what, if left to themselves, common men would call common sense."[22] The exception is the philosophy of Saint Thomas: "the Thomist philosophy is nearer than most philosophies to the mind of the man in the street."[23]

In the hands of the Wizard of Paradox, in other words, Catholicism—so often represented as a clear example of esoteric doctrine imposed by authority on a populace sunk in superstition—becomes, with very considerable plausibility, the representative of the sanity and common sense of the ordinary man, and the only basis for radical reform.

Only with reservations, then, can one describe Chesterton as a "Catholic" political thinker. In one sense this is certainly appropriate, for throughout his life he insisted that without a foundation in true religion, the social and political ideals for which he campaigned could never be secure. However, although his own political outlook was closely linked to his understanding of Catholicism, it was a very long way indeed from the kind of right-wing authoritarianism asserted by some Catholic political thinkers and supported in practice by a great many popes.

Chesterton was aware of the complexities of his position, which are explored in one of his prewar novels, *The Ball and the Cross.* This is the story of a series of attempts by two men to fight a duel on religious grounds, and their pursuit by authorities who regard such conduct not only as a breach of the peace but as insane. The two are James Turnbull, the radical and progressive editor of *The Atheist,* and Evan MacIan, a Scottish Highlander who is a Catholic and a romantic Jacobite. In the course of the book (whose plot is complicated by overlaid symbolisms), each is tempted by a vision of the realization of something like the society he has longed for. First MacIan dreams that he is summoned (in a flying-ship) to fight for the return of the King and the re-establishment of secular and religious authority. At first, as the ship passes over London, he is thrilled by the spectacle of order and discipline, and the splendid gleaming weapons of the cavalry ranged about St. Paul's Cathedral. But then he sees a soldier strike an old man without reason, and the angel ("Lucifer") who is his conductor justifies this with sophistries about discipline being more important than individual justice. MacIan cannot accept this, and revolts.

Turnbull is also summoned in the visionary flying-ship, but to fight for the Revolution; as they pass over London he sees vast areas going up in flames, and is told that there lived the unemployables, who were deficient in class consciousness, and whom the Revolution is therefore wiping out in the interests of efficiency and progress. Turnbull, too, revolts at this sacrifice of real human beings to totalitarian orthodoxy. One of the messages of the allegory, in other words, is that a social theory that exalts any principle—whether traditional order or revolutionary justice—at the expense of ordinary individual human beings, is always the work of the devil.

In this novel, then, the right-wing authoritarianism that might superficially be taken for "Catholic" political doctrine is shown to be as false as left-wing elitist tyranny. Chesterton indeed claims that the spirit of humanity and justice which can alone resist all tyranny rests upon Christianity, but this true Christianity is represented by a solitary and totally unworldly monk, Michael, rather than by any institutional and political Church. A similar repudiation of "Catholic" politics seems to be implied in *The Return of Don Quixote,* published four years after he joined the Roman Catholic Church. At the end of the novel the two heroines, in love respectively with Braintree the syndicalist and Herne the reviver of medieval kingship, both become Roman Catholics, having realized that the principles of justice and honor represented by their men can find their place only in relation to true religion. However, in spite of this insight into the religious foundations of a good social order, and these personal conversions, there is not the slightest suggestion that what is needed is a Catholic political movement, nor any kind of activity by the Church as an institution.

2. Populism and Fascism

In the years following Chesterton's conversion to Roman Catholicism, the problems of reconciling personal and institutional Catholic politics became acute. For the Roman Catholic Church as an institution had a justified reputation as the opponent of everything that could be called liberalism. Ever since the French Revolution the Church had tended, in spite of the efforts of radical Catholic thinkers, to side with the kings, the aristocrats, and their police forces against political reforms; and just about the time when Chesterton entered the Church, its leaders were beginning to negotiate with the new Right—Fascism. The Italian case illustrates the tension between the radical possibilities that others besides Chesterton could discern in Catholic Christianity, and the conservatism of Catholic institutions.

In 1919 a Sicilian priest, Don Luigi Sturzo, founded the Partito Popolari, a Catholic populist party, calling for agrarian reform and appealing to the proletariat and poor peasants of the South. So effective was this appeal that the party immediately gained a substantial number of parliamentary seats, and the Popolari looked for a time like serious rivals of Mussolini and his Fascists. However, after Mussolini's ascent to power Sturzo found himself not only threatened by the Fascists, but dropped by the leaders of his Church, who had begun the process of compromise with the new regime that eventually produced the Concordat in 1929. Sturzo was driven into exile.

Chesterton visited Italy just about the time when the Concordat was signed, and on his return wrote a book about Italy and Fascism, *The Resurrection of Rome*. He made it clear that his own initial sympathies had been with the Popolari, and reiterated constantly that he did not approve of many aspects of Fascism, and would not himself have chosen it. Nevertheless, he felt obliged to approach it in a spirit of open-minded enquiry and to see what there was to be said for Mussolini.

The book is a very odd piece of work. Where Chesterton's usual style is concise, emphatic, and to the point, this book is overlong, loaded with qualifications and explanatory appendices, and clogged by an atmosphere of deep embarrassment. It was very much as an Englishman that Chesterton had gone to Rome: an Englishman of Protestant upbringing, although a Catholic convert, and of liberal convictions, although determined to be fair to Mussolini. The fact is, his qualified defense of Fascism in the latter part of the book has a flavor very similar to his attempt at the start to convince himself and his readers that there is some value in Italian baroque statuary. He himself understood and shared the English distaste both for writhing marble bodies and for strong-arm methods in politics, and wrote about each with the air of one who had suspended his natural distaste just long enough to see the point of them, if not actually like either of them.

He agreed with Mussolini's critics that the Fascists had done evil things. However, he argued that all revolutions have always done so, and that if one were to reject Fascism on grounds of violence alone one must also condemn the French Revolution, the Irish Nationalist movement, and many other causes with which English liberals had always sympathized. In Mussolini's favor he maintained that his government had shown an independence of the rich, and a willingness to coerce employers, that would have horrified those English Tories who liked to call for "strong government." He reiterated that a truly republican government, in the hands of equal citizens, would be best, but maintained that a popular dictator was better than an oligarchy of plutocrats. After pages of qualifications and cautions, he uttered a cry from the heart: "I wish there were in the world a real white flag of freedom, that I could follow, independent of the red flag of Communist or the black flag of Fascist regimentation. By every instinct of my being, by every tradition of my blood, I should prefer English liberty to Latin discipline."[24] But he concluded sadly that no such liberal option existed: for England, which had once been the home of personal liberty—though not of equality or social justice—had now lost even this claim to grace, as she succumbed to bureaucratic regulation and official harassment of the poor.

In his final section on Fascism, Chesterton expressed doubts about its chances of stability: "The intellectual criticism of Fascism is really this; that it appeals to an appetite for authority, without very clearly giving the authority for the appetite."[25] He was unconvinced by the defenses of minority rule put forward by such writers as Charles Maurras (of the Action Française, the French equivalent of Fascism), for, as he pointed out, such doctrines provide no test of which minority should rule. A majority vote can be a test acceptable to everyone, since there cannot be more than one majority, whereas there may be an indefinite number of organized minorities, each convinced of its fitness to rule and none possessing any basis for legitimacy. "The common complaint against the Blackshirts is that they exercise too much authority; the real complaint against them is that they have too little."[26]

It is clear from this book that Chesterton was far from regarding himself as a Fascist, and that his enthusiasm for Mussolini was of a very muted kind. However, some of his associates on *G.K.'s Weekly* took a more extreme position, to the extent of supporting Mussolini's invasion of Ethiopia.* Maisie Ward prints a letter from Chesterton to a friend distressed by the line taken by the paper, in which he explained that he had been away on holiday at the time, and affirmed his own condemnation of the invasion.[27] What is difficult to decide is whether his willingness

* After Chesterton's death, his paper became markedly right-wing.

to see some good in Mussolini reflects simply charity toward his Catholic coreligionists, or—as is sometimes suggested—a natural affinity between his own brand of populism and fascism: a built-in drift toward the Right which his conversion to Roman Catholicism merely confirmed.

There are certain grounds for such a claim. Let us begin by stating the affinities baldly. First, Chesterton's political thought appealed to emotions that were the staple of fascist rhetoric: the love of home and country, and the glory of fighting for them. Furthermore, he shared the Fascist disillusionment with parliamentary government, which he regarded as merely a mask for plutocracy. Worst of all—though a trait more associated with the French or German Right than with Mussolini's Fascism—his hostility to both plutocracy and Bolshevism was strongly marked by anti-Semitism.

Let us now consider Chesterton's position in more detail, taking first the issue of parliamentary democracy. His disillusionment with the British parliamentary system dated from before World War I, and had a great deal to do with the views and experiences of his brother and Belloc. These two had declared in *The Party System* that the supposed opposition between the parties was a charade played for the mystification of the public by a small clique of interrelated families, a governing oligarchy that could be penetrated only by those rich enough to buy political influence. The Marconi affair convinced them, and Chesterton as well, that government was corrupt and the situation hopeless, since all members of the great governing clique could be counted upon to cover up for one another regardless of their party label.

This sense of the hopelessly unbridgeable gap between the people and their "representatives" pervades all Chesterton's political writings and much of his fiction, and received particularly vivid expression in a series of stories published in 1922, *The Man Who Knew Too Much*. Horne Fisher, the man of the title, is a disillusioned idealist related to all the aristocratic families, acquainted with the seamier side of public life, and therefore too knowledgeable to suppose any reform possible. In each of the crimes described in the book, Fisher can identify the criminal but cannot bring him to book, since he is too highly placed to be punishable. In the first story, a man has been shot while on his way to expose another for corruption; his death will be treated as a motor accident because his murderer is a friend of the Prime Minister, and a rich man paying into party funds in return for his peerage. (To emphasize what a closed world the governing circles are, Chesterton has their intimates calling the Prime Minister and other dignitaries by absurd nicknames such as "Puggy" and "Jinks.")

One particularly striking story describes the youthful experience that first disillusioned Fisher. Although the scion of a prominent Liberal family, Fisher has hitherto shown little interest in politics. One day, however, on hearing that a Radical is to contest a local county seat on a platform of opposition to feudal squirearchy and support for county councils and social reform, he decides to stand, too, on a more realistic platform of his own. He points out that the local squire is far from being a remnant of feudal aristocracy, but is in fact a foreign plutocrat who owes his place entirely to his dubious financial operations; further, that the local population of agricultural laborers do not want county councils but the land itself. This program of Distributism and antiplutocracy is immensely popular with the electorate, but runs up against the secret rules of politics. Fisher's own family, exasperated by his attempts to uncover the squire's seamy past, join forces with the Tory interest to get him out of the way; in a terrible moment of disillusionment, Fisher discovers that the man doing the corrupt squire's dirty work is none other than his own brother.

The picture of politics given in *The Man Who Knew Too Much* is a hopelessly dark one. Just as a Marxist might maintain that parliamentary democracy is merely a façade for bourgeois class rule, so Chesterton, taking a typical populist stance, saw in it the mask of the plutocrat. According to his own view of English history, England had been ruled by the rich ever since they grew fat on the spoils of the Reformation in the sixteenth century. During their heyday in the eighteenth and nineteenth centuries, these oligarchs had at least acquired the limited but real virtues of gentlemen, to set against their unchallenged exploitation of the poor.

"It was the very soul of our old aristocratic policy that even a tyrant must never figure as a tyrant. He may break down everybody's fences and steal everybody's land, but he must do it by Act of Parliament and not with a great two-handed sword. And if he meets the people he's dispossessed, he must be very polite to them and enquire after their rheumatism. That's what kept the British Constitution going— enquiring after the rheumatism."[28]

But in his own time it seemed to him—as to so many of his contemporaries—that a new breed of international plutocrats, born of large-scale capital, international finance, and imperialist operations like the South African war, were buying out the older aristocracy and holding the supposed democracies to ransom. His writings are haunted by this sense of plutocrats behind the scenes, pulling the wires to make politicians dance.

In one of his essays, printed in *A Miscellany of Men,* he elaborated this view of plutocracy:

The evil enigma for us here is not the rich, but the Very Rich. The distinction is important; because this special problem is separate from the old general quarrel about rich and poor.... The special problem today is that certain powers and privileges have grown so world-wide and unwieldy that they are out of the power of the moderately rich as well as of the moderately poor. They are out of the power of everybody except a few millionaires.... In the old normal friction of normal wealth and poverty I am myself on the Radical side. I think that a Berkshire squire has too much power over his tenants; that a Brompton builder has too much power over his workmen; that a West London doctor has too much power over the poor patients in the West London Hospital.

But a Berkshire squire has no power over cosmopolitan finance, for instance. A Brompton builder has not money enough to run a Newspaper Trust. A West London doctor could not make a corner in quinine and freeze everybody out. The merely rich are not rich enough to rule the modern market. The things that change modern history, the big national and international loans, the big educational and philanthropic foundations, the purchase of numberless newspapers, the big prices paid for peerages, the big expenses often incurred in elections—these are getting too big for everybody except the misers: the men with the largest of earthly fortunes and the smallest of earthly aims.[29]

He often complained that the supposedly free press was in the pockets of a few very rich men, and he noted frequently how much newspaper space was devoted to flattering the rich, commonly in terms of fatuous praise of their "simplicity of life." And whereas the old flatterers of kings had generally attributed to them totally improbable virtues, the modern flatterers of the rich were more subtle, apparently describing them in straightforward terms, but giving the impression that even the most mundane and uninteresting characteristic of a rich man becomes glamorous through contact with his wealth.

Given Chesterton's views on the rich, he had mixed feelings about his visit to America. Here, on the one hand, was capitalism at its most untrammeled, New York hung with neon signs in which the rich advertised their monopolies. On first seeing the lights of Broadway, he exclaimed, "What a glorious garden of wonders this would be, to anyone who was lucky enough to be unable to read."[30] On the other hand America, unlike England, possessed a real democratic ideal with which plutocracy came into constant collision. In England the traditional deference to the aristocratic rich spread its mantle over the new rich who could so easily buy peerages. But in America reverence for successful men was tempered with a democratic suspicion of millionaires. Chesterton reported how he had been in Oklahoma during a cause célèbre—the trial of a girl, for the murder of a millionaire senator who had seduced her. He was surprised to find that the dead man's wealth and public position, instead of exonerating him, made him more suspect in the mind of the public.

To put the matter shortly, England recognises a criminal class at the bottom of the social scale. America also recognises a criminal class at the top of the social scale. In both, for various reasons, it may be difficult for the criminals to be convicted; but in America the upper class of criminals is recognised. In both America and England, of course, it exists.[31]

Chesterton believed, then, that the curse of his time was rule by the rich, and that parliamentary democracy—at any rate, in its English form of the party system—was hopelessly inadequate to resist this. His own political ideal was democracy of the most direct and equal kind; but like many another populist, he preferred a popular dictatorship ruling openly to what he saw as the alternative—plutocrats pulling strings behind the scenes.

As he made abundantly clear, the cornerstone of his own political thought was his unshakable belief in the equality of men. Consequently, his ideal was democracy in its most direct and Rousseauian sense. He wrote, for instance, in *A Miscellany of Men:*

Self-government arose among men (probably among the primitive men, certainly among the ancients), out of an idea which seems now too simple to be understood. The notion of self-government was not (as many modern friends and foes of it seem to think) the notion that the ordinary citizen is to be consulted as one consults an Encyclopedia. He is not there to be asked a lot of fancy questions, to see how he answers them. He and his fellows are to be, within reasonable human limits, masters of their own lives.... The men of the valley shall decide whether the valley shall be devastated for coal or covered with corn and vines; the men of the town shall decide whether it shall be hoary with thatches or splendid with spires.[32]

And he followed this passage by discussing the dramatic changes then taking place in and around his own little town of Beacons-field. On the one hand, the outskirts of London were advancing into the country, while on the other, the ownership of the land was passing "into the hands of men who are always upstarts and often actually foreigners." Over these real changes in the conditions of their own lives, the local people had no control at all; yet every five years a general election called for their views on things totally irrelevant. As Chesterton remarked in the course of another discussion of the problem: "We have not got real Democracy when the decision depends upon the people. We shall have real Democracy when the problem depends upon the people. The ordinary man will decide not only how he will vote, but what he is going to vote about."[33] However, he was prepared to admit that such genuine democracy was possible only in very small communities, and he went on to say something that for the modern reader smacks of fascism: "Given this difficulty about quite direct democracy over large areas, I think the nearest thing to democracy is despotism."[34] We must look more closely at what he meant by this.

It is important to realize that Chesterton was not one of the rather hysterical worshippers of "strong men" so common among the intelligentsia of his time. On the contrary, he was an English Liberal with a deep respect for law and liberty; his conviction that in some circumstances despotism was preferable to parliamentary government, was reached with a full sense of the shock that it must give to English Liberals. He stated his case most elaborately in *The Resurrection of Rome,* where, as a preliminary to appraising the claims of Mussolini, he first discussed the idea of a Republic. For him, the essence of the republican idea was that all citizens should be equal, and government public and impartial. The English, he thought, had grown so used to government by the rich and for the rich, that they could not imagine anything else: they could not conceive of laws that applied equally to rich and poor, or that government offices might be anything other than the monopoly of the rich. They would, for instance, be shocked by the French military regulation according to which gentlemen and laborers alike had to serve their time in the ranks. Within a real republic, he maintained, only the rank of citizen is important, and the government stands above all classes. Furthermore, "this civil ideal is not in all cases inconsistent with monarchy, but it is, in my opinion, inconsistent with aristocracy."[35]

The case against parliamentary democracy, Chesterton thought, was that it meant untrammeled rule by the rich, whereas the case for a popular despotism was that it might be strong enough to impose its laws on rich and poor alike. The kind of popular despotism that he had in mind was chiefly represented in history by Bonapartism, which he often defended. However, his reflections on America suggested an even more congenial example: Andrew Jackson, "the one great democratic despot of modern times; the Napoleon of the New World." Chesterton maintained that

the energy of that great man was largely directed towards saving us from the chief evil which destroys the nations today. He sought to cut down, as with a sword of simplicity, the new and nameless enormity of finance; and he must have known, as by a lightning flash, that the people were behind him, because all the politicians were against him.[36]

Chesterton also had some sympathy with the old Tory notion of the patriot king, who represents the true interests of the people against the oligarchs. In his *Short History of England*, which was consciously directed against the orthodox Whig version, he stressed that the "tyrannical" Stuarts had tried to stop the enclosures that robbed the English poor of their land, and that the triumph of liberty after the 1688 Revolution had in effect meant unrestrained rule by rich landlords. While persistently denouncing the British upper classes, he had great respect for the royal family, particularly King George V, and shared the popular English enthusiasm for royalty. In the stories of his later years such as *Four Faultless Felons* and *The Paradoxes of Mr. Pond,* sympathetic figures of kings sometimes appear—not, indeed, as charismatic despots, but as wise and moderate men who stand outside the particular interests of opposed classes, and represent the people without being tainted by the corruption of professional politicians. Whether or not Chesterton thought that, in Britain or anywhere, these dreams of political salvation through a revived monarchy were feasible, they at least indicate his belief that a popular leader, even if not elected, might be more representative than a parliamentary party.

Of the various aspects of Chesterton's political thought that might be considered fascist, the hardest nettle to grasp is his anti-semitism. There has in fact been considerable dispute about whether or not he *was* anti-semitic. He himself denied the suggestion on several occasions, and his biographer, Maisie Ward, not only denies it, but prints a kind of testimonial from an American rabbi: "Indeed I was a warm admirer of Gilbert Chesterton.... He as Catholic, I as Jew, could not have seen eye to eye with each other ... but I deeply respected him. When Hitler came, he was one of the first to speak out."[37] What, then, was his position?

First, Chesterton was not a racist, and would have been the last to believe in Nazi doctrines of racial purity. (Nazism seemed to him, indeed, simply a revival of the abominable Prussianism that he had denounced so uninhibitedly during World War I.) Nor did he ever suggest or support any persecution of Jews. His own reasoned views on the Jewish question were of a kind that many of his Jewish contemporaries could have accepted. He was not being merely paradoxical when he called himself a Zionist. His basic claim was that Jews were different from the Englishmen, Frenchmen, or Germans among whom they lived. Descent, religion, history, and culture all contributed to give them a special character; and nothing but a disservice to them was done by liberals who blandly pretended that the difference did not exist. He stated his position most clearly in a chapter at the end of *The New Jerusalem,* the travel book that was the product of his visit to Palestine: "Jews are Jews; and as a logical consequence... they are not Russians or Roumanians or Italians or Frenchmen or Englishmen."[38]

Chesterton's point was a version of the argument about nationalism that we have already looked at: that as long as this basic difference were recognized, it would be possible to come to terms with it; but that if Jews tried to disguise themselves as Englishmen or Frenchmen, nothing could come of it but distrust and hostility. At times he played with the idea that Jews might be more acceptable if their separate identity were made visible by their being obliged to wear Eastern dress:

I have often felt disposed to say: let all liberal legislation stand, let all literal and legal civic equality stand; let a Jew occupy any political or social position which he can gain in open competition; let us not listen for a moment to any suggestions of reactionary restrictions or racial privilege. .... But let there be one single-clause bill; one simple and sweeping law about Jews, and no other. Be it enacted ... that every Jew must be dressed like an Arab.[39]

It is impossible to read this without being chilled by the recollection of the Nazis' Nuremberg Laws; but of course Chesterton was quite innocent of any such connection, and had no idea of making such separate dress a mark of shame and an incitement to mob violence.

What he considered the special national character of the Jews seemed to him to arise from their landlessness, and he therefore believed that the problem could be solved by giving them a national home of their own. He remarked that in some respects the Jews resembled the gypsies:

Both races are in different ways landless, and therefore in different ways lawless. For the fundamental laws are land laws. In both cases a reasonable man will see reasons for unpopularity, without wishing to indulge any taste for persecution. In both cases he will probably recognise the reality of a racial fault, while admitting that it may be largely a racial misfortune. That is to say, the drifting and detached condition may be largely the cause of Jewish usury or Gipsey pilfering; but it is not common sense to contradict the general experience of Gipsey pilfering or Jewish usury.[40]

This analogy could not be pushed very far, however, for

the Jewish problem differs from anything like the Gipsey problem in two highly practical respects. First, the Jews already exercise colossal cosmopolitan financial power. And second, the modern societies they live in also grant them vital forms of national political power. Here the vagrant is already as rich as a miser, and the vagrant is actually made a mayor.[41]

Chesterton pointed to the Rothschild family to make his point that Jewish power was incompatible with national interests.

The Jewish problem can be stated very simply after all. It is normal for the nation to contain the family. With the Jews the family is generally divided among the nations. This may not appear to matter to those who do not believe in nations, those who really think there ought not to be any nations. But I literally fail to understand anybody who does believe in patriotism thinking that this state of affairs can be consistent with it. It is in its nature intolerable, from a national standpoint, that a man admittedly powerful in one nation should be bound to a man equally powerful in another nation, by ties more personal and private even than nationality. Even when the purpose is not any sort of treachery, the very position is a sort of treason.[42]

The Zionist answer—that, given a land of their own, the Jews would settle into being a nation—appealed to Chesterton, with one proviso. He understood and sympathized with the fears of the Palestinian Arabs that the Jews would come in and establish a plutocracy to exploit them, and he remarked that a Jewish state would be successful only when there were Jewish laborers as well as Jewish bankers.

One may object that, contrary to Chesterton's belief, Jews do *not* usually remain separate from the nations among which they live, and that the international Rothschilds were far outnumbered by the genuinely assimilated Jews who really were English, American, or whatever nationality. Yet his position so far is at any rate a defensible one, and one that has been held by many Zionist Jews themselves. If Chesterton had stuck to arguments at this level, there would have been no grounds for calling him anti-semitic. Unfortunately, there was another and much less defensible side to his writing about Jews, a side with much more resemblance to the scurrilous anti-semitic journalism of France. For Chesterton's books, particularly his fiction, are full of cheap jokes about pawnbrokers' noses and sinister figures of Jewish plutocrats. At times there is even a suggestion of a worldwide Jewish conspiracy akin to the fantasies of the Nazis, particularly after the Jewish plutocrats were joined in the demonology by the Bolshevik Jews of Russia: "The cosmopolitan Jews who are the Communists in the East will not find it so very hard to make a bargain with the cosmopolitan Jews who are Capitalists in the West."[43]

For a modern Chestertonian this kind of thing creates not only embarrassment but a genuine problem of understanding. True, the same cheap jokes about Jewish names and Jewish noses pervade the literature and journalism of the period, but that could hardly excuse so self-conscious and idiosyncratic a writer as Chesterton. True, he really did have Jewish friends and seems to have got on well with the Jews that he met; but this makes it all the more difficult to understand how he could have continually insulted their community in print. By the standards of the time his anti-semitism was very mild—but why was it there at all? He was not a neurotic, or a man of violent hatreds whose prejudices could be explained in terms of psychological compensation. (Some of the people who wrote anti-semitic letters to the *New Witness* clearly came into this category.) It would be convenient if one could ascribe Chesterton's failings in this respect to the influence of Belloc: though this will not do as a general explanation, it is certain that in one instance, over the Dreyfus case, Belloc did convert Chesterton from the standard liberal defense of the prisoner to a more uncertain stance.[44]

Perhaps Chesterton's attitude can only be made explicable by means of a modern parallel. In a great many parts of the world today it is fashionable to be anti-American, and left-wingers in particular tend to consider hostility to America and all it is taken to stand for as one of the marks of their commitment. When an American embassy somewhere is stormed, or a suspected C.I.A. agent shot, left-wingers generally see in such an event less the particular individuals who have suffered than the symbolic humiliation of a mighty oppressor. Not only neurotic extremists bursting with half-suppressed violence, but also genuinely humanitarian idealists allow themselves to respond in this way. Now let us try to imagine that some terrible defeat or disaster were to befall America—say, that she were to be virtually wiped out by Russian H-bombs, and the tiny surviving population were to be helpless refugees. To those looking back from the other side of such a disaster, the radical rhetoric of anti-Americanism would seem as unspeakably indecent as do the casual anti-semitic jokes of Chesterton, after the Nazi holocaust. To radicals like Chesterton, the economic and political power of the Jews all over the Western world seemed as secure and unchallengeable as does that of America now; and the idea of a Final Solution seemed as incredible then as does the destruction of America now. The jokes about pork and noses, which we read as bullying taunts against the weak, were often meant by their writers as brave gestures defying the mighty.

Let us now reach some conclusions about Chesterton's relation to fascism. It is clear that he had points in common with some aspects of fascism and with some of the people who supported it; also that, at any rate for a time, he felt more sympathy with Mussolini's regime than with either Communists or defenders of the English parliamentary system. However, it is also clear that he was by no means a whole-hearted supporter of the fascists, and that there were important differences between his views and theirs.

Here we run up against the inevitable problem of what is to count as fascism. No useful purpose will be served by trying to define so vague and ambiguous a term; but when we consider Italian Fascism, Nazism, and the various right-wing groups in France, it is obvious that they share one prominent characteristic with which Chesterton had nothing at all in common: elitism. Fascists shared Chesterton's suspicion of parliaments, but often for very different reasons. One of the central identifiable strands in intellectual fascism is denunciation of the weak and humanitarian doctrines of the French Revolution: liberty, equality, fraternity. A common fascist objection to parliamentary government was that it was democratic, that it gave power to the common herd, whereas Chesterton's objection was precisely that it was *not* democratic.[45] Among the theoreticians of fascism there was much Nietzschean exaltation of supermen, and corresponding contempt for the mass; and it is important to realize that this is completely absent from Chesterton's thought. In *Heretics,* one of his earliest works, Chesterton made fun of Nietzsche's romanticism about heroes by comparing him to the writers of snobbish novelettes: "Nietzsche and the *Bow Bells Novelettes* have both obviously the same fundamental character; they both worship the tall man with curling moustaches and herculean bodily power, and they both worship him in a manner which is somewhat feminine and hysterical."[46]

Elsewhere in the same book Chesterton wrote perceptively of Nietzsche's contempt for the common herd. His remarks occur in the context of a discussion of the advantages of small communities over large ones.

It is not fashionable to say much nowadays of the advantages of the small community. We are told that we must go in for large empires and large ideas. There is one advantage, however, in the small state, the city, or the village, which only the wilfully blind can overlook.

141

The man who lives in a small community lives in a much larger world. He knows much more of the fierce varieties and uncompromising divergences of men. The reason is obvious. In a large community we can choose our companions. In a small community our companions are chosen for us.[47]

Chesterton suggested that the modern intellectual flees the small community because he cannot stand the strain of facing up to humanity in all its rampant variation:

He is forced to flee, in short, from the too stimulating society of his equals—of free men, perverse, personal, deliberately different from himself. . . .

Of course, this shrinking from the brutal vivacity and brutal variety of common men is a perfectly reasonable and excusable thing as long as it does not pretend to any point of superiority. . . . Fastidiousness is the most pardonable of vices; but it is the most unpardonable of virtues. Nietzsche, who represents most prominently this pretentious claim of the fastidious, has a description somewhere . . . of the disgust and disdain which consume him at the sight of the common people with their common faces, their common voices, and their common minds. As I have said, this attitude is almost beautiful if we may regard it as pathetic. Nietzsche's aristocracy has about it all the sacredness that belongs to the weak. When he makes us feel that he cannot endure the innumerable faces, the incessant voices, the overpowering omnipresence which belongs to the mob, he will have the sympathy of anybody who has ever been sick on a steamer or tired in a crowded omnibus. Every man has hated mankind when he was less than a man. . . . But when Nietzsche has the incredible lack of humour and lack of imagination to ask us to believe that his aristocracy is an aristocracy of strong muscles or an aristocracy of strong wills, it is necessary to point out the truth. It is an aristocracy of weak nerves.[48]

Chesterton was himself blessed with strong nerves, and did not feel this impulse to shrink from the common herd and then exalt his shrinking into superiority. On the contrary, he did not think of mankind as "the common herd" at all. There is a revealing passage in one of his essays when, while discussing Charlotte

Brontë, he remarks on the truth of her shabby governesses who hide fires of passion, and goes on to point out that the endless suburbs of London, so often condemned for mere drab repetition, do *not* contain an indistinguishable mass of the vulgar: "Each of these men is supremely solitary and supremely important to himself. Each of these houses stands in the centre of the world."[49]

In view of Chesterton's sense of the vital importance of every single human being, it is not surprising that his qualified support for Mussolini should have been so uncertain and embarrassed. In truth, his kind of egalitarian populism was no more compatible with fascism than with dictatorial communism or with plutocracy. As is the case with many (perhaps most) thinking people, Chesterton never found any political party or movement that he could support wholeheartedly—not even Distributism— so that choosing sides in particular cases resolved itself into a choice of evils. The complexities of his own stance result from the fact that he saw his populist ideals menaced not by *one* enemy, but by three, two of them perversions in practice of ideals that were attractive in theory.

In the first place there was the danger that Chesterton deemed the greatest in those years before World War I, the danger of a Servile State with an apparatus of official regulation pressing upon the poor, rendering them more helpless than ever in the face of their capitalist masters. This danger was summed up by the Mental Deficiency Act, under which anyone—provided, of course, that he were not rich or powerful—could be locked up for life on the word of two doctors and on the flimsiest of pretexts. Over and over again in Chesterton's writings the preoccupation with this most comprehensive threat to liberty recurs, and it is not accidental that characters in so many of his novels are at various times threatened with imprisonment in asylums.[50]

However, besides the danger of a totalitarian state run by scientifically minded officials in the interests of plutocrats, Chesterton was equally well aware of two other sources of oppression, from the Right and from the Left. The danger that the high-minded ideals of socialism might in practice produce tyranny became a reality after the Russian Revolution, when refugees from Bolshevism testified to the cruelty of a regime that had nominally inherited the idealism of the Left. Yet when, in *The Return of Don Quixote,* Chesterton reconsidered some of the symbolic themes explored earlier in *The Ball and the Cross,* his emphasis was very much less upon the dangers from the Left—represented in a sympathetic form in Braintree—than upon the pitfalls of right-wing romanticism. Michael Herne, the shortsighted and unworldly medievalist, shares MacIan's dream of the restoration of medieval kingship and social order; but as in the case of MacIan's vision from the flying-ship, this blind romanticism in practice permits the ruling class to strike down insubordination by ordinary men. Since romantic right-wing views were current in some Catholic circles, it is significant that Chesterton emphasized their dangers in a novel published not long after his conversion, and at a time when the leaders of his new church were countenancing Fascism in Italy.

Far from being in any sense a typically Catholic political thinker, Chesterton occupied a position of great practical complexity. Before World War I, when neither tyrannical revolution nor romantic reaction seemed particularly imminent, it was natural for him to stand with the Left, especially the syndicalists, in attacking official invasions of the rights of the poor. After the war, however, in spite of his continued sympathy with the labor movement, many things conspired to make him more suspicious of the Left, and more ready to give a cautious hearing to the Right. One was certainly his conversion to Roman Catholicism, which brought him into a right-wing ambience; another was the triumph of Bolshevism in Russia. However qualified Chesterton's sympathy with Mussolini might be, he was at any rate quite sure that fascism of the Italian type was better than Bolshevism. If he had lived to see the full development of Nazism—which he detested from the start—and the alliance between Hitler and Mussolini, it is virtually certain that he would have changed his stance again; compared with Stalin on the one hand and the Axis dictators on the other, even the corrupt and ramshackle British parliamentarianism would have seemed worth defending.

In his latter years, indeed, in spite of his adherence to radical slogans inherited from earlier days, he seems to have sunk into a sad conservatism that was as far from fascism as it was from the militant Left. In *The Ball and the Cross* there had been two central political characters, Left and Right, complementing one another; significantly, in *The Return of Don Quixote* there is also a third, the ironic and apolitical Douglas Murrel. Perhaps Murrel— with his common sense, his lack of fanaticism, his sympathy with the common people, and his unwillingness to take sides—really represents Chesterton's own later views more closely than any of his other characters. For one thing Murrel, like Chesterton himself, is very English, and asserts a peculiarly English con- servatism against the un-English ideological politics of the others. His comment on Herne's fictional authoritarianism perhaps helps illuminate Chesterton's own views on Mussolini's Fascism. For Murrel seems to suggest that that sort of thing may be all very well for the Latin races, but is not suited to the peculiar vices and virtues of Englishmen:

You said just now that we wanted a strong man in England. Now I should say that the one place where we never have wanted a strong man is England.... These high-handed ways don't suit us a bit, either revolutionary or reactionary. The French and the Italians have frontiers and they all feel like soldiers. So the word of command doesn't seem humiliating to them; the man is only a man, but he commands because he is the commander. But we are not democratic enough to have a dictator. Our people like to be ruled by gentlemen, in a general sort of way. But nobody could stand being ruled by one gentleman. The idea is too horrible.[51]

Epilogue:
Chesterton Today

In this book we have considered in successive chapters four complementary aspects of Chesterton's populism. We looked at his belief in the worth, dignity, and common sense of the common man, and then at his opposition to all social schemes and arrangements that sanctioned dominion by a supposedly enlightened elite. We saw that his own recipe for giving ordinary men self-determination and independence was to settle families on their own land, and to cut down political units to a size compatible with democracy. This concern for the common man and hatred of elitist regimentation was intrinsically bound up with his opposition to progress as it is commonly understood, that is, to industrialism, urbanization, increases in the size of political and economic units, administrative complexity, and formal education. Unlike most of his generation, Chesterton insisted that such "progress" was not an inevitable fate, and that men could avert it if they chose to do so. These elements add up to a fairly coherent political outlook that is thoroughly radical while having nothing in common with Marxism, social democracy, or welfare liberalism. What, then, has been the fate of this alternative radicalism since Chesterton's day?[1]

As we have seen, Chesterton's populism made very little impact in his own time, and for many years after his death the climate of opinion was quite unsympathetic to it. From the 1930s to the 1960s, all the various forms of influential radicalism were pledged to the same goal of industrial progress led by an elite vanguard of one type or another, and it was sufficient to say that views like Chesterton's were "reactionary" to condemn them out of hand. If the fashionable radicalism of the 1930s was Communism, the idealistic liberalism that dominated Western policies after World War II was no less committed to an elitist conception of progress, with vanguards of scientific and technical experts trying to extend the blessings of development all over the world. The initial reaction against this form of liberalism, the New Left, was if anything more frankly elitist than old-style proletarian Marxism, and was just as oriented toward progress.

Since the 1960s, however, there have been some interesting changes in the Western climate of opinion. For the first time in over a century, there is now widespread and influential questioning of the desirability of "progress." Although this new disillusionment is widely diffused over the industrial world—or at least over the noncommunist parts of it—it derives much of its impetus from recent crises in the most thoroughly developed country of all, the United States. It has many components. Part of the trouble is economic: it has become increasingly apparent that permanent poverty persists on a vast scale in highly developed countries, even amid the wealth of the United States. Furthermore, still greater numbers have found themselves out of work in the recent recession—a reminder that the larger the scale of industrial enterprises, the more workers are at risk when the economy is in trouble.

Political crises have reinforced the economic malaise. Vietnam and Watergate, and the subsequent reverberations of the Lockheed investigation, have been stark reminders of how much power modern governments have, how disastrously it may be misused, and how little guarantee the people have that those who rule in their name are to be trusted. Meanwhile, the social costs of modernization have become increasingly obvious, as the social problems of communities escalate with their size, and urban crime rates make the centers of modern cities more dangerous than jungles. Above all, the great awakening of recent years has been to the environmental consequences of industrialization. People in the developed countries have at last become aware of the pollution of air and rivers, the degeneration of food, the dangers of radiation and other by-products of progress, and have realized that irreplaceable natural resources are being used up in an utterly prodigal way. Furthermore, the warnings of conservationists were made dramatically relevant by the oil crisis of 1973, which demonstrated how dependent the advanced industrial countries are on constant supplies of fossil fuel, and also how politically vulnerable we are as a direct result of our very level of development.

Along with this recent and very sudden collapse of popular faith in the necessary goodness of progress, we have seen in Western countries a simultaneous loss of faith in the experts who are supposed to be directing our course. It has dawned on many people that, in a number of conspicuous cases, the crucial decisions made by experts have actually been worse than those that would have been made by any random group of ordinary people. What committee of people, chosen by lot from the inhabitants of any district, would have decided to build a nuclear reactor, with all its dangers of radiation, near their homes and families, or to spend millions of pounds on supersonic Concordes to shatter their greenhouses and their babies' sleep? If the inhabitants of slum-clearance areas had been consulted about town-planning, would they have leveled whole districts to build tower blocks and then discovered belatedly, as the experts have done, that such blocks are uninhabitable? Experiences of this kind have been giving rise to a new desire for democracy, based on the sound conviction that experts are no more sensible or trustworthy than anyone else.

Therefore it is not surprising that, although the tendency

toward ever larger political, social, and economic units continues under its own momentum, a countermovement toward the small, manageable, and controllable should have arisen. Britain is an interesting example of this dialectic: just at the moment when the United Kingdom was being dragged into the European Economic Community by her leaders, and was reluctantly ratifying their fait accompli in a referendum, resurgent nationalism in Scotland was confounding all the political predictions, and threatening a breakup of Britain of which Chesterton would surely have approved.

Another symptom of the current opposition to progress, loss of faith in industrial society, concern for conservation, and desire for self-determination, is the new drift back to the land. Besides the innumerable attempts at agrarian communes by youthful dropouts, increasing numbers of people are emulating the Distributists in trying to make themselves self-sufficient on small plots of land. The trend is typified in Britain by the periodical *Resurgence,* started in 1966. Its most noted contributors, Leopold Kohr and E. F. Schumacher, set the tone of the magazine, which advocates smaller political, economic, and social units; conservation instead of pollution; small holdings, intensively cultivated, instead of large-scale farming run as a business enterprise; intermediate technology to help small farmers and craftsmen, instead of industry to throw them out of work; sympathy with the peasants of the Third World rather than with its modernizing elites.

Interestingly, some of the contributors to *Resurgence* actually quote Chesterton as a precursor,[2] and clearly these radical conservationists have a great deal in common with him. What is much less clear, however, is whether their spectrum of attitudes could be called populist. As we have seen, Chesterton's own populism was of a somewhat ambiguous nature. Although he defended values characteristic of peasants, he was not representing a peasantry but trying to create one; and although he claimed that he spoke to and for the actual common people of England, there is not much ground—apart from the undeniable popularity of his books—for maintaining that he did so. His populism has in fact two distinguishable sides to it: on the one hand, a faith in the common sense of ordinary people; and on the other, a commitment to a specific social ideal of small, self-governing peasant nations.

Since Chesterton's time this combination of agrarian values with an appeal to the people has become much less tenable, since the vast majority of the people of Britain, as of all other industrial countries, are now thoroughly urbanized, state-educated, and influenced by the media. It would be rash to assume that devotion to the simple virtues of country life is widespread among the populace of the United Kingdom; the conservationists, like the Distributists before them, are in fact largely drawn from the intellectual middle class. Unlike Chesterton, on the other hand, radicals of the *Resurgence* type tend to be too much in the tradition of humanitarian internationalism to sympathize with such spontaneously popular movements as do exist in Britain. They applaud Scottish and Welsh nationalism, insofar as it makes for smaller political units, but they are unlikely to have much in common with the other strikingly populist upsurge in current British politics: the Little England nationalism, with racist overtones, whose most famous spokesman has been Mr. Enoch Powell. The newly articulate political feeling against colored immigration into Britain is very much a grass-roots political phenomenon, and one which the leaders of all major parties have done their best to discourage. It is also precisely the kind of thing that makes many intellectuals dislike populism, and regard it as a halfway house on the road to fascism. It is interesting to speculate on what Chesterton's views might have been, had he lived into the era of large-scale immigration and Powellism. Presumably, in view of his attitude to the Jews, he would have opposed harassment of immigrants, but favored restriction of immigration and voluntary repatriation—a position which is theoretically coherent, but extraordinarily hard to distinguish from racism in practice.

At the present time, then, both sides of Chesterton's populism —both the reaction against industrial society, and the grassroots, antielitist nationalism—are very much alive, although in England, as in most of the industrial countries, they tend to be disconnected from one another. Insofar as the intellectual conservationists have sympathy with the prejudices of ordinary people, their populist solidarity tends to be directed toward the rather distant populace of Third World peasants. The recent revival of interest in populism, after so many years when it was dismissed as merely reactionary, is in fact largely due to the emergence, either in the Third World itself or in relation to it, of forms of radicalism that have many parallels with Russian populism. The stress in these cases is on opposition to modernization, when modernization means an indiscriminate copying of advanced industrial societies that is imposed by urban elites on a rural population. Instead, the critics of industrialism appeal for the preservation or gradual building up of peasant society.

In an interesting recent book belonging to this school,[3] the American sociologist Peter Berger has attacked what he calls the "myths" of progress propagated in the Third World by both Right and Left: their claims that the sufferings of the present generation, whether as uprooted slum dwellers on the fringes of Westernized cities, or as forcibly collectivized comrades under revolutionary regimes, will eventually result in prosperity and happiness for all. He compares these enforced hardships with the human sacrifices made to the bloodthirsty gods of ancient Mexico, on pyramids which the peasants toiled to build, and for which they also ultimately supplied the victims. Professor Berger states flatly: "Policies for social change are typically made by cliques of politicians and intellectuals with claims to superior insights. These claims are typically spurious."[4] He devotes particular attention to deflating the elitist assumption, common to

---

151

idealists of both Right and Left, that they are enlightened, and that it is their business to "raise the consciousness" of the peasants whom they wish to help: "It is, in principle, impossible to 'raise the consciousness' of anyone, because all of us are stumbling around on the same level of consciousness—a pretty dim level."[5]

Instead, Professor Berger puts forward as a crucial value what he calls "cognitive respect"—the recognition that every person knows his own world and his own experience better than anyone else possibly can, and that the benevolent outsider who comes in to try to help must, at the very least, accord the object of his benevolence the dignity of being *listened* to, not treated as a benighted idiot. Professor Berger's type of new and more respectful benevolence toward the "underdeveloped" reflects recent and rueful discoveries that peasants themselves may sometimes know more about how to make things grow on their own land than technical experts sent in from America. Some of these experts have been discovering that there was a reason for apparently inefficient agricultural practices, and that the wholesale adoption of modern methods can be ruinous. As the Russian populists learned in the course of their ill-fated attempt to go to the people, the first thing to do is not to talk to the peasants, but listen to them.

The parallel with the Russian populists brings forcibly to mind the great difficulty of intellectual populism. The young Russian idealists, dreaming of harmonious fraternity in communion with nature, had their illusions rudely shattered when they encountered real peasants: the people in whom they placed their faith did not share their ideals. Such is the problem of any populism that is not purely a grass-roots articulation of popular grievances: it must combine, with a specific social ideal of popular life, faith in the real common people who may or may not subscribe to that ideal. Even Chesterton—who genuinely shared a great many popular tastes and prejudices, from love of adventure stories to distrust of foreigners—encountered this problem when his ideal of Distributism failed to gather popular support. Clearly, this difficulty is absolutely central to populism as an ideology. Those who put their trust in the simple people usually assume that the people will share their particular ideals and judgments, whereas the people's wishes may well turn in a different direction—or, most likely of all, prove to be multifarious, confused, and self-contradictory.

We must conclude, then, that populism as an ideology is incoherent. However, it would be a gross error to suppose that, having identified this incoherence at its heart, we can dismiss populism as invalid. For the sobering truth is that *all* the great political ideals are similarly incoherent.[6] Consider only the perpetual problem that lies at the heart of liberalism—and not just of its "positive" variety—namely, that it is apparently necessary to use coercion and restrict freedom in order to create freedom; or the Marxist dilemma of how a highly developed society with socialized production is to overcome alienation. Populism is not in fact any more incoherent than other more academically respectable political ideologies: it has simply been more neglected and less influential. This neglect is unfortunate, because populist traditions enshrine human values that other ideologies have tended to neglect—values that could profitably be brought to bear on the making of political decisions. Few have articulated those values more clearly and persuasively than G. K. Chesterton.

Notes

Unless otherwise stated, all the books mentioned below were published in Great Britain. When the work cited is not the original edition, the date of the original edition follows the title in parentheses.

Chapter 1

1. G. K. Chesterton, *The Common Man,* Sheed and Ward, 1950, p. 38.
2. For a variety of attempts at definition, see *Populism: Its Meanings and National Characteristics,* ed. G. Ionescu and E. Gellner, Weidenfeld and Nicholson, 1969.
3. *Ibid.,* p. 166.
4. *Ibid.,* p. 171.
5. See e.g. Richard Wortman, *The Crisis of Russian Populism,* Cambridge University Press, 1967. For a more sympathetic summing up, see Sir Isaiah Berlin's Introduction to Franco Venturi, *The Roots of Revolution,* Weidenfeld and Nicholson, 1960.
6. For the various stages of the controversy, see the articles collected in Theodore Saloutos, ed., *Populism: Reaction or Reform,* American Problem Studies, Holt, Rinehart and Winston, New York, 1968.
7. See e.g. "The Queer Feet" and "The Sign of the Broken Sword" (*The Innocence of Father Brown*); "The Resurrection of Father Brown," "The Arrow of Heaven," and "The Oracle of the Dog"

(*The Incredulity of Father Brown*); "The Blast of the Book" (*The Scandal of Father Brown*).

8. *Autobiography*, Hutchinson, 1936, p. 13.
9. *Ibid.*, p. 115.
10. *Heretics*, John Lane, 1905, p. 22.
11. *G. K. Chesterton: A Criticism*, Alston Rivers, 1908, p. 60.
12. Donald Read, *Edwardian England, 1901–15*, Harrap, 1972, p. 90.
13. Maisie Ward, *Gilbert Keith Chesterton*, Sheed and Ward, 1944 (hereafter referred to as "Ward"), p. 254.
14. *Orthodoxy* (1908), Fontana, 1961, p. 45.
15. *Autobiography*, p. 129.
16. Ward, p. 252.
17. For a careful account of this tangled affair, see Ward, Ch. 19.
18. *Autobiography*, p. 247.
19. Maisie Ward, *Return to Chesterton*, Sheed and Ward, 1952, p. 130.

Chapter 2

1. *Orthodoxy* (1908), Fontana, 1961, p. 11.
2. *Ibid.*, p. 47.
3. *Ibid.*, p. 115.
4. Maisie Ward, *Return to Chesterton*, Sheed and Ward, 1952, p. 83.
5. *The Defendant* (1910), J. M. Dent, 1940, p. 24.
6. *Orthodoxy*, p. 9.
7. *Ibid.*, p. 10.
8. *Ibid.*, p. 22.
9. *Ibid.*, p. 32.
10. *Ibid.*, p. 45.
11. *Ibid.*, p. 89.
12. *Ibid.*, p. 104.
13. *Ibid.* p. 106.
14. *Robert Browning*, Macmillan, 1903, p. 1.
15. Chesterton must be rolling with funeral mirth at the attempts that have been made, by well-meaning but humorless scholars, to give

his own fiction academic respectability through comparisons with Kafka and Proust. See e.g. Hugh Kenner, *Paradox in Chesterton,* Sheed and Ward, 1948; P. N. Furbank, "Chesterton the Edwardian," in *G. K. Chesterton: A Centenary Appraisal,* ed. John Sullivan, Elek, 1974.

16. *Charles Dickens,* Methuen, 1906, pp. 87–89.
17. Ward, p. 157.
18. *Charles Dickens,* pp. 104–07.
19. *What's Wrong with the World* (1910), Cassell, shilling ed., 1912, p. 257.
20. *William Cobbett,* Hodder and Stoughton, 1925, pp. 146–48.
21. *Ibid.,* p. 216.
22. *Ibid.,* p. 218.
23. Ward, p. 540.

Chapter 3

1. *What's Wrong with the World* (1910), Cassell, Shilling ed., 1912, pp. 61–64.
2. Ward, p. 262.
3. Speech at the second New Witness conference, reported in the *New Witness,* Vol. II, No. 36, July 10, 1913.
4. See Maurice Bruce, *The Coming of the Welfare State,* Batsford, 1961; José Harris, *Unemployment and Politics,* Oxford University Press, 1972; J. R. Hay, *The Origins of the Liberal Welfare Reforms, 1906–1914,* Macmillan, 1975.
5. C. Booth, *The Life and Labour of the People of London,* Macmillan, 1892–97; B. S. Rowntree, *Poverty: A Study of Town Life,* Macmillan, 1901.
6. Bruce, *The Coming of the Welfare State,* p. 190.
7. Bernard Semmel, *Imperialism and Social Reform,* Allen and Unwin, 1960, p. 62.
8. Harris, *Unemployment and Politics,* especially Chapter 3.
9. *Ibid.,* p. 254.
10. *England a Nation,* ed. Lucian Oldershaw, R. Brimley Johnson, 1904.
11. *Ibid.,* p. 82.

12. Harris, *Unemployment and Politics,* p. 314.
13. Quoted in Donald Read, *Documents from Edwardian England,* Harrap, 1973, p. 202.
14. *New Age,* Vol. II, 1907–08, pp. 189–90, p. 250.
15. *What I Saw in America* (1922), Da Capo Press, New York, 1968, p. 20.
16. *What's Wrong with the World,* p. 3.
17. *Ibid.,* p. 32.
18. *Ibid.,* p. 47.
19. *Ibid.,* p. 56.
20. *Ibid.,* p. 59.
21. *Ibid.,* p. 66.
22. *Ibid.,* p. 48.
23. *Ibid.,* p. 78.
24. *Ibid.,* p. 91.
25. *Ibid.,* p. 95.
26. *Ibid.,* p. 105.
27. *Ibid.,* p. 104.
28. *Ibid.,* p. 99.
29. *Ibid.,* p. 82.
30. *Ibid.,* p. 108.
31. *Ibid.,* p. 131.
32. *Ibid.,* p. 132.
33. Ward, p. 178.
34. *What's Wrong with the World,* p. 133.
35. *Ibid.,* p. 198.
36. *Ibid.,* p. 204.
37. *Ibid.,* p. 247.
38. *Ibid.,* p. 248.
39. *Ibid.,* p. 273.
40. *Ibid.,* p. 279.
41. Ward, p. 264.
42. *New Witness,* Vol. I, No. 6, December 12, 1912. Burt's scientific reputation has recently been seriously impugned—he has in fact been posthumously accused of scientific fraud.
43. *British Journal of Sociology,* Vol. I, 1950, p. 157.
44. Ada Chesterton, *The Chestertons,* Chapman & Hall, 1941, p. 253.
45. *New Witness,* Vol. IX, No. 246, July 19, 1917.

46. Ward, p. 273.
47. "Wine and Water," *The Collected Poems of G. K. Chesterton*, Methuen, 1933, p. 200.
48. Harris, *Unemployment and Politics*, p. 307.
49. See Anne Vernon, *A Quaker Businessman*, Allen and Unwin, 1958, p. 138.
50. *George Bernard Shaw*, (1909), John Lane, popular ed., 1914, p. 179.
51. *Autobiography*, p. 126.
52. Article by Sidney Webb in *The Times* of London, 1906, quoted in Donald Read, *Edwardian England*, Harrap, 1972, p. 21.
53. *Memories*, 1908, quoted in C. P. Blacker, *Eugenics: Galton and After*, Gerald Duckworth, 1952, p. 111.
54. *Darwinism, Medical Progress and Eugenics*, quoted in Semmel, *Imperialism and Social Reform*, p. 48.
55. C. W. Daniel, 1931.
56. *Ibid.*, p. 42.
57. *Ibid.*, p. 93.
58. Harris: *Unemployment and Politics*, p. 46.
59. E.g. Vincent MacNabb's article in the *New Witness*, Vol. II, No. 45, September 11, 1913. See also L. S. Hearnshaw, *A Short History of British Psychology, 1840–1940*, Methuen, 1964, pp. 151–54.
60. *Eugenics and Other Evils*, Cassell, 1922, p. 12.
61. *Ibid.*, p. 63.
62. *Ibid.*, p. 76.
63. *Ibid.*, p. 137.
64. *Ibid.*, p. 141.
65. *Ibid.*, pp. 105–07.
66. *Ibid.*, p. 164.
67. In his sister-in-law Ada, the redoubtable Fleet Street journalist who wrote under the name of J. K. Prothero, Chesterton had an example immediately before his eyes of—in his terms—a thoroughly "masculine" woman. Perhaps the antagonism between her and Chesterton's domestic and retiring wife Frances may have had something to do with his very sweeping assertions. See Ada Chesterton, *The Chestertons*, 1941.
68. See Anthony Smith, *The Human Pedigree*, Allen and Unwin, 1975, for a very useful general account.

69. For a classic statement of this position, see S. M. Lipset, *Political Man*, Heinemann, 1960, especially Chapter 4.
70. *Charles Dickens*, Methuen, 1906, p. 231.
71. *Eugenics and Other Evils*, p. 177.

Chapter 4

1. Chesterton's translation from Du Bellay, *Collected Poems*, Methuen, 1933, p. 179.
2. *All Things Considered* (1908), Methuen, 13th ed., 1919, p. 80.
3. *What's Wrong with the World* (1910), Cassell, shilling ed., 1912, p. 215.
4. *Autobiography*, Hutchinson, 1936, p. 32.
5. *A Miscellany of Men* (1912), Methuen, 6th ed., 1930, p. 43.
6. *The Outline of Sanity* (1926), Bernhard Tauchnitz, Leipzig, 1927, p. 62.
7. *Ibid.*, p. 11.
8. *Irish Impressions*, Collins, 1919, pp. 27–30.
9. *The Outline of Sanity*, p. 132.
10. *Ibid.*, p. 127.
11. *Ibid.*, p. 140.
12. G. Ionescu, "Eastern Europe," in G. Ionescu and E. Gellner, eds., *Populism: Its Meanings and National Characteristics*, Weidenfeld and Nicholson, 1969.
13. *Heretics*, John Lane, 1905, p. 79.
14. *Twelve Types*, A. L. Humphreys, 1902, p. 24.
15. *The Outline of Sanity*, p. 185.
16. See for instance the current British periodical, *Resurgence*.
17. *The Outline of Sanity*, p. 98.
18. See for example, "The Fool," *A Miscellany of Men*, pp. 121–28.
19. "The Other Kind of Man," *A Miscellany of Men*, pp. 221–27.
20. *The Outline of Sanity*, p. 175.
21. See J. M. Winter, *Socialism and the Challenge of War*, Routledge and Kegan Paul, 1974, passim.
22. *Alarms and Discursions* (1910), Methuen, 3rd ed., 1924, p. 77.
23. Chesterton's somewhat schizoid attitude can be seen in one of his public comments on the General Strike in *G.K.'s Weekly*, May

22, 1926, p. 160: "And while we ourselves have always preferred the policy of small property, we have never hesitated to defend the proletarian organization as the only actual defense of the classes without property."

24. *The Return of Don Quixote*, p. 52.
25. For an interesting analysis of its interwoven symbolisms, see Ian Boyd, *The Novels of G. K. Chesterton*, Elek, 1975, pp. 115–38.
26. Maisie Ward, *Return to Chesterton*, Sheed and Ward, 1952, pp. 228–32.
27. "The Wrong Incendiary," *A Miscellany of Men*, p. 75.
28. *The Napoleon of Notting Hill*, John Lane, 1904, p. 134.
29. *England a Nation: Being the Papers of the Patriots' Club*, ed. Lucian Oldershaw, R. Brimley Johnson, 1904.
30. *Ibid.*, p. 15.
31. *The Napoleon of Notting Hill*, p. 106.
32. W. R. Titterton: *G. K. Chesterton: A Portrait*, Douglas Organ, 1936, pp. 44–45.
33. Cecil Chesterton, *G. K. Chesterton: A Criticism*, Alston Rivers, 1908, p. 39.
34. *The Everlasting Man*, Hodder and Stoughton, 1925, p. 80.
35. *Heretics*, p. 174.
36. *What I Saw in America* (1922), Da Capo Press, New York, 1968, p. 2.
37. *Ibid.*, p. 7.
38. *Ibid.*, p. 13.
39. *The Napoleon of Notting Hill*, pp. 40–41.
40. Quoted by P. N. Furbank in "Chesterton the Edwardian," in *G. K. Chesterton: A Centenary Appraisal*, ed. John Sullivan, Elek, 1974, p. 20.
41. Cecil Chesterton, *G. K. Chesterton: A Criticism*, p. 39.
42. *The Resurrection of Rome*, Hodder and Stoughton, 1930, pp. 218–19.
43. *The Napoleon of Notting Hill*, p. 119.

Chapter 5

1. *The Ballad of the White Horse* (1911), quoted from *The Collected Poems of G. K. Chesterton*, Methuen 1933, p. 233.

2. *What I saw in America* (1922), Da Capo Press, New York, 1968, p. 246.

3. *G. K. Chesterton: A Criticism.*

4. *Eugenics and Other Evils,* Cassell, 1922, p. 92.

5. *The Outline of Sanity* (1926), Bernhard Tauchnitz, Leipzig, 1927, p. 165.

6. *Ibid.,* p. 168.

7. *Ibid.,* p. 169.

8. *Autobiography,* Hutchinson, 1936, pp. 293–94.

9. *What's Wrong with the World* (1910), Cassell, shilling ed., 1912, p. 33.

10. *Heretics,* John Lane, 1905, p. 33.

11. *Autobiography,* p. 223.

12. *The Thing* (1929), Unicorn Books, 1939, p. 16.

13. *What I Saw in America,* p. 305.

14. *Fancies Versus Fads* (1923), Methuen, 4th ed., 1930, pp. 179–85.

15. *Ibid.,* p. 183.

16. *A Short History of England,* Chatto and Windus, 1917, pp. 79–80.

17. *Fancies Versus Fads,* pp. 86–92.

18. *Fancies Versus Fads,* p. 90.

19. *Ibid.,* p. 91.

20. *St. Thomas Aquinas,* Hodder and Stoughton, 1933, p. 26.

21. *Ibid.,* p. 34.

22. *Ibid.,* p. 172.

23. *Ibid.,* p. 173.

24. *The Resurrection of Rome,* Hodder and Stoughton, 1930, p. 283.

25. *Ibid.,* p. 286.

26. *Ibid.,* p. 289.

27. Ward, p. 549. On the relation between the Roman Catholic Church and Italian fascism, see Carlo Falconi, *The Popes in the Twentieth Century,* Weidenfeld and Nicholson, 1967, and Anthony Rhodes, *The Vatican in the Age of the Dictators, 1922–45,* Hodder and Stoughton, 1973.

28. Douglas Murrel in *The Return of Don Quixote,* Chatto and Windus, 1927, p. 262.

29. *A Miscellany of Men* (1912), Methuen, 6th ed., 1930, pp. 141–42.
30. *What I Saw in America*, p. 33.
31. *Ibid.*, p. 191.
32. *A Miscellany of Men*, p. 9.
33. *Ibid.*, p. 37.
34. *What I Saw in America*, p. 243.
35. *The Resurrection of Rome*, p. 257.
36. *What I saw in America*, p. 75.
37. Ward, p. 228.
38. *The New Jerusalem*, Thomas Nelson, 1920, p. 221.
39. *Ibid.*, p. 227.
40. *Ibid.*, p. 232.
41. *Ibid.*, p. 233.
42. *Ibid.*, p. 234. Though Chesterton does not make the point, it is obvious that this objection would apply even more strongly to the much-intermarried European royal families.
43. *What I Saw in America*, p. 247.
44. Ward, p. 117.
45. In an essay "On the One-Party System" published early in the 1930s (*Avowals and Denials*), he remarked on the bewilderingly backhanded way in which the notion of the "Party system," which he and his friends had put forward in earlier days, was becoming generally accepted: for those who now denounced parliamentary democracy as a sham seemed to suppose that the one-party state was somehow an *improvement*. Chesterton stressed instead that totalitarian states had exactly the same defects as oligarchic parliamentarianism, but in a much exaggerated form.
46. *Heretics*, p. 197.
47. *Ibid.*, p. 180.
48. *Ibid.*, p. 185.
49. *Twelve Types*, A. L. Humphreys, 1902, p. 13.
50. E.g. *The Ball and the Cross, Manalive, The Return of Don Quixote, The Poet and the Lunatics*, etc.
51. *The Return of Don Quixote*, p. 261.

Epilogue

1. For a strongly argued defense of Chesterton's relevance today, see Patrick Cahill, "Chesterton and the Future of Democracy," in John Sullivan, ed., *G. K. Chesterton: A Centenary Appraisal,* Elek, 1974.
2. See e.g. Geoffrey Ashe, "A Prophet Ignored," *Time Running Out? Best of Resurgence,* ed. M. North and S. Kumar, PRISM, Dorchester, 1976, p. 119.
3. Peter Berger, *Pyramids of Sacrifice,* Allen Lane, 1976.
4. *Ibid.,* p. 13.
5. *Ibid.,* p. 13.
6. For a brilliant demonstration that all possible alternative utopias are equally objectionable, see Ernest Gellner; "Prepare to meet thy doom," in his *Contemporary Thought and Politics,* Routledge and Kegan Paul, 1974.

Bibliography

Unless otherwise stated, all the books mentioned below were published in Great Britain.

I. Chesterton's Works

This chronological list includes only those works particularly relevant to the present study. For a more comprehensive list, see John Sullivan, *G. K. Chesterton: A Bibliography* (1958) and *Chesterton Continued* (1968). References in the text are usually to the first edition of the work, but where a later edition has been used this is indicated in parentheses below.

1900 *The Wild Knight and Other Poems.* G. Richards
1901 *The Defendant.* (J. M. Dent, 1940)
1902 *Twelve Types.* A. L. Humphreys
1902 *Robert Browning.* Macmillan
1904 "The Patriotic Idea." In *England a Nation,* edited by Lucian
　　　　Oldershaw, R. Brimley Johnson.
　　　　The Napoleon of Notting Hill. John Lane
　　　　G. F. Watts. Barker
1905 *The Club of Queer Trades.* Hodder and Stoughton
　　　　Heretics. John Lane
1906 *Charles Dickens.* Methuen
1908 *The Man Who Was Thursday.* Arrowsmith
　　　　Orthodoxy. (Fontana, 1961)
　　　　All Things Considered. Methuen (13th ed., 1919)

1909 *George Bernard Shaw.* John Lane (popular ed., 1914)
Tremendous Trifles. Methuen

1910 *The Ball and the Cross.* Wells Gardner
What's Wrong with the World. Cassell (shilling ed., 1912)
Alarms and Discursions. Methuen 3rd ed., 1924)

1911 *The Innocence of Father Brown.* Cassell
The Ballad of the White Horse. Methuen
Manalive. Arrowsmith

1912 *A Miscellany of Men.* Methuen (6th ed., 1930)
The Victorian Age in Literature. Williams and Norgate

1914 *The Wisdom of Father Brown.* Cassell
The Flying Inn, Methuen
The Barbarism of Berlin. Cassell

1915 *The Crimes of England.* Palmer and Hayward

1917 *A Short History of England.* Chatto and Windus

1919 *Irish Impressions.* Collins

1920 *The New Jerusalem.* Thomas Nelson

1922 *Eugenics and Other Evils.* Cassell
The Man Who Knew Too Much. (Darwen Finlayson, 1961)
What I Saw in America. (Da Capo Press, New York, 1968)

1923 *Fancies Versus Fads.* Methuen (4th ed., 1930)
St. Francis of Assisi. Hodder and Stoughton (People's Library ed., 1924)

1925 *The Everlasting Man.* Hodder and Stoughton
Tales of the Long Bow. (Bernhard Tauchnitz, Leipzig, 1925)
William Cobbett. Hodder and Stoughton

1926 *The Outline of Sanity.* (Bernard Tauchnitz, Leipzig, 1927)
The Incredulity of Father Brown. Cassell

1927 *Collected Poems.* (Methuen, 1933)
The Return of Don Quixote. Chatto and Windus
Robert Louis Stevenson. Hodder and Stoughton
The Secret of Father Brown. Cassell

1928 *Generally Speaking.* Methuen

1929 *The Thing.* Sheed and Ward (Unicorn Books ed., 1939)
The Poet and the Lunatics. Cassell

1930 *Come to Think of It.* Methuen
The Resurrection of Rome. Hodder and Stoughton
Four Faultless Felons (Darwen Finlayson, 1964)

1933 *St. Thomas Aquinas.* Hodder and Stoughton
      All I Survey. Methuen
1934 *Avowals and Denials.* Methuen
1935 *The Scandal of Father Brown.* Cassell
      The Well and the Shallows. Sheed and Ward
1936 *Autobiography.* Hutchinson
1937 *The Paradoxes of Mr. Pond.* (Darwen Finlayson, 1963)
1950 *The Common Man.* Sheed and Ward

II. Books about Chesterton

Barker, Dudley. *G. K. Chesterton.* Constable, 1973.

Boyd, Ian. *The Novels of G. K. Chesterton.* Elek, 1975.

Chesterton, Ada. *The Chestertons.* Chapman & Hall, 1941.

Chesterton, Cecil. *G. K. Chesterton: A Criticism.* Alston Rivers, 1908.

Kenner, Hugh. *Paradox in Chesterton.* Sheed and Ward, 1948.

Sullivan, John, ed. *G. K. Chesterton: A Centenary Appraisal.* Elek, 1974.

Titterton, W. R. *G. K. Chesterton: A Portrait.* Douglas Organ, 1936.

Ward, Maisie. *Gilbert Keith Chesterton.* Sheed and Ward, 1944. (This is the authorized biography, and most useful source. It is referred to in notes as "Ward.")

————. *Return to Chesterton.* Sheed and Ward, 1952.

III. Other Books

Armstrong, Charles Wickstead. *The Survival of the Unfittest.* Daniel, 1931.

Armytage, W.H.G. *Heavens Below.* Routledge and Kegan Paul, 1961.

Belloc, Hilaire. *The Servile State.* T. N. Foulis, 1912.

Berger, Peter. *Pyramids of Sacrifice.* Allen Lane, 1976.

Bibby, H. C. *Heredity, Eugenics and Social Progress.* Left Book Club, 1939.

Blacker, C. P. *Eugenics: Galton and After.* Gerald Duckworth, 1952.

Bruce, Maurice. *The Coming of the Welfare State.* Batsford, 1961.

Burt, Sir Cyril. "The Trend of National Intelligence." In *British Journal of Sociology,* Vol. I, 1950.

Cole, G. D. H., and Postgate, Raymond. *The Common People, 1946–1938*. Methuen, 1945.

Emy, H. V. *Liberals, Radicals and Social Politics, 1892–1914*. Cambridge University Press, 1973.

Falconi, Carlo. *The Popes in the Twentieth Century*. Weidenfeld and Nicholson, 1967.

Gellner, Ernest. *Contemporary Thought and Politics*. Routledge and Kegan Paul, 1974.

Glass, S. T. *The Responsible Society: The Ideas of the English Guild Socialists*. Longmans, 1966.

Harris, José. *Unemployment and Politics*. Oxford University Press, 1972.

Hay, J. R. *The Origins of the Liberal Welfare Reforms, 1906–1914*. Macmillan, 1975.

Hearnshaw, L. S. *A Short History of British Psychology, 1840–1940*. Methuen, 1964.

Ionescu, G., and Gellner, E., *Populism: Its Meanings and National Characteristics*. Weidenfeld and Nicholson, 1969.

Koss, Stephen. *Nonconformity in Modern British Politics*. Batsford, 1975.

Lansbury, George. *My Life*. Constable, 1928.

Morris, A. J. A., ed. *Edwardian Radicalism, 1900–1914*. Routledge and Kegan Paul, 1974.

North, M., and Kumar, S. eds. *Time Running Out? Best of Resurgence, PRISM,* 1976.

Pitt-Rivers, George. *Weeds in the Garden of Marriage*. Noel Douglas, 1931.

Read, Donald. *Documents from Edwardian England*. Harrap, 1973.
———. *Edwardian England, 1901–15*. Harrap, 1972.

Rhodes, Anthony. *The Vatican in the Age of the Dictators, 1922–45*. Hodder and Stoughton, 1973.

Saloutos, Theodore, ed. *Populism: Reaction or Reform?* American Problem Studies. Holt, Rinehart and Winston, New York, 1968.

Semmel, Bernard. *Imperialism and Social Reform*. Allen and Unwin, 1960.

Smith, Anthony. *The Human Pedigree*. Allen and Unwin, 1975.

Speaight, Robert. *The Life of Hilaire Belloc*. Hollis and Carter, 1957.

Swinnerton, Frank. *The Georgian Literary Scene*. J. M. Dent, 1951.

Venturi, Franco. *The Roots of Revolution*. Weidenfeld and Nicholson, 1950.

Vernon, Ann. *A Quaker Businessman*. Allen and Unwin, 1958.

Winter, J. M. *Socialism and the Challenge of War*. Routledge and Kegan Paul, 1974.

Wortman, Richard. *The Crisis of Russian Populism*. Cambridge University Press, 1967.

Index